THE **13** BIGGEST MISTAKES PARENTS MAKE
and how to avoid them

What parents can do to help their children
be more self-reliant and successful

Steven J. Anderson

The Yes Press
Dallas, TX
www.theyespress.com

Library of Congress Cataloging-in-Publication Data

Anderson, Steven J.
The 13 Biggest Mistakes Parents Make
and how to avoid them
What parents can do to help their children
be more self-reliant and successful

p.   cm.
Includes index.
ISBN 1882306538

1. Parenting   2. Youth motivation   3. Interpersonal relations

Library of Congress Control Number 2003112046

Publisher: The Yes Press
Dallas, TX
www.theyespress.com

First Edition

Cover design by Jesse Brande

Dedication

To Dad and Mom -

Arthur and Janice Anderson

You wrote the solutions to the "13 Biggest Mistakes" by your example in successfully raising all seven of us. Thanks for giving us a great start in life and for continuing your amazing example as parents, grandparents and great grandparents.

Without your continuous encouragement and tireless efforts in editing, correcting and proofing every word of this book, it would have never come about.

Thanks for making this book happen.

Thanks for making me happen!

Love,

#7 – The "caboose", your "lease on youth"!

Reference Guide

Several resources are mentioned throughout this book that may be useful as you read.   For more information, contact the following:

The Book:

For comments, questions and additional resources on
<u>The 13 Biggest Mistakes Parents Make and How to Avoid Them</u>:
www.mistakesparentsmake.com

Eagle "U":

Youth Success Seminars helping high school and college students get a 7-year career head start.

1-888-7-Eagle-U   or (888) 732-4538
www.eagleu.com

The Author:

For more information on the author, speaking engagements and additional works:
www.stevenjanderson.com

The Publisher:

The "Yes" Press
www.theyespress.com

Contents

The Problem: Parental Mistakes Become
Young People's Problems   1

Mistake 1: Creating and Fostering
the Entitlement Attitude   7

Mistake 2: Failing to Develop a Proper
Deserve Level   19

Mistake 3: Failing to Recognize That Your Children
Will Not Likely Rise Above What You
Expect of Them   39

Mistake 4: Having a House with No "Walls"   53

Mistake 5: Being a Victim of Approval Addiction
and Passing It on to Your Children   67

Mistake 6: Accepting Average   85

Mistake 7: Having a House Divided   95

Mistake 8: Failing to Understand and Act on
the Feather Philosophy   111

Mistake 9: Providing Dependable
"911 Emergency Rescue"   129

Mistake 10: Following the "Do As I say, Not As
I Do" Philosophy   145

Mistake 11: Failing to Teach That Right Is Right
and Wrong Is Wrong   157

Mistake 12: Failing to Put Money in the
Proper Perspective   169

Mistake 13: Thinking One Size Fits All   185

THE PROBLEM
Parental Mistakes Become Young People's Problems

As parents we try not to make mistakes, but we act and react mostly from our own bringing up and what we have otherwise learned. Out of our total experience we develop a mind fix that we pass on to our children. Some things are very helpful but others are not always the best for the individual personalities individual children have and for the different ways they respond to motivation.

This book has been written to help parents avoid making the mistakes that cause young people to become

        ✓   unfocused,
        ✓   directionless,
        ✓   indecisive,
        ✓   unproductive,
        ✓   and unsuccessful.

The tragedy is that these problems are not usually evident until many years have passed and young people become victims of what we call the "Catfish Catastrophe."

The Catfish Catastrophe

Being a "catfish" may be alright for some fish, but catfish habits are not really acceptable for humans. For instance, catfish are bottom feeders. They swim at the lowest depths of the river or lake and feed mostly on leftovers - things other fish or people have ignored or discarded. In its daily journey, a catfish swims along until it bumps into some object such as a rock whereupon it changes direction. Then it hits a sunken log and changes direction again.

Since it is dark down where the catfish searches for food, it is fortunate that he has extended whiskers to keep him from bumping too harshly into the objects encountered. However, his whiskers don't make him any more efficient. They only enable him to keep wandering around even when he is "up in the night" still hunting for food.

Too many young people make the most important decisions in life in the same fashion as the catfish. They move along in some random direction until something gets in their pathway. Not having decided upon a definite course, they pick up on whatever presents itself, often things that are just available. Whether it be friends, habits, values, beliefs, a job, a career, a significant other or vocational activities, far too many young people start out in life "catfish style" with no direction. Many continue through life in the same fashion, and the result can be such things as mental depression, divorce, and career disaster.

How did we learn about the catfish catastrophe and its causes? For more than ten years we have worked with thousands of young high school and college-age students from throughout North America in week-long courses we call Eagle University or Eagle "U" for short.

During these seminars we discovered some of the mistakes that have been made by those guiding young people that could have been avoided. Here are two typical examples of catfish catastrophes:

Catfish Case Study #1: Mike went through high school as an average student doing whatever was required. He went to college because most of his friends were going. He got involved on campus and even held some leadership positions. He went through four years of undergraduate study in business because it was a popular major at the school. As a senior it finally occurred to him that he would soon need to go out into the real world, get a job, and start a career. So he went to the career placement center, looked at the job interview board and signed up to interview with whomever came to the school to recruit.

He accepted the first job offer he got with a major soft-drink company in its management development program. He had stars in his eyes. And why not, this was a large, successful, aggressive company, seemingly providing the opportunity to move eventually into a high paying executive position.

Six months out of college, Mike was working thirteen-hour days stocking grocery store shelves. He soon got an advancement in his job responsibilities, however, when he was allowed to start driving the delivery truck as well as stock the shelves!

Mike began to wonder when he was ever going to have an opportunity to use his college education. The theory was that he was learning how the company operated from the ground up. Intellectually, he understood that. But he just had no tolerance for this repetitive non-challenging daily work. Since he wasn't sure he wanted to do whatever was up the line on a prospective career path, he quit.

Because he couldn't decide what he wanted to do next, he did what many intelligent college grads do who can't make a career decision - he went back to school. This time it was graduate school. It was much more comfortable there. For two more years the only decisions he had to make were about when to do all of his homework.

Near the end of his two years of graduate school, reality struck again and he had to find a real job. Back to the career center he went. This time he got a job with a major brand name consumer goods company as a member of a brand management team. Again he was into menial tasks that didn't much challenge his intellect. So after about two years he quit.

Let's do the math here:
18 months in his first job
+ a six month hiatus before graduate school
+ two years of graduate school
+ two years in his second job.

That adds up to six years out of college and Mike was out of work, out of energy and totally lost. All he knew was that there were two jobs he did not want to do. Many call this job experience. I call it a waste of six very productive years of life that could have been totally avoided.

Finally after about a year of temporary jobs, Mike found his way into a small company and he loved it. He found something he enjoyed doing. But he had spent seven years bumping into obstacles and changing direction while he was finding out by trial and error just what it was he wanted to do.

Mike was lucky. Many, if not most, never find a real direction in life personally or professionally. But what if Mike could have avoided his catastrophe altogether and found the right direction for himself much earlier in life? What if he had learned to avoid the biggest mistakes that contribute to the catfish catastrophe? Most of those mistakes are made by well-meaning parents who raise their "catfish" to be like all the other "catfish" who tend to be confused in youth and on into adulthood. There are some well-tested ways of avoiding this. What you can do to help young people avoid this catastrophe is what this book is all about.

Catfish Case Study #2: Richie was the son of a wealthy medical doctor - an anesthesiologist. It was a family tradition, or at least the father's mind-set, that every son should have a career in what is classed as a profession - not just a job. Since Dad was paying all the bills and gave Richie just about anything he wanted, any attempt on Richie's part to go in a career direction other than what his father viewed as appropriate was met with veiled financial threats from his father. Because Richie was living it up on Dad's dole, he just went along with his father's desires for his future.

Richie got by scholastically in college, spending most of his time partying and running up big bills on Dad's credit card. Under his father's direction and by his father's influence, Richie was accepted into law school. He made it through law school, sent his resume out and was recruited by a prestigious law firm. The schooling had been interesting, but Richie was totally miserable with the daily work in the law office. There was nothing about it that he liked. So he quit and followed the same pattern as catfish number one - he went back to school.

He got a Master's degree in taxation, thinking he could be an expert in tax law. He followed that path and got a good paying job with a west coast law firm. He found the work to be about as uninteresting to him as the previous work was. Feeling consigned to a professional life of misery, he began surviving from day to day until he could accrue enough vacation time or get at least a three-day weekend during which he could get away from it all and go skiing. It is possible, if not probable, that Richie will spend the rest of his life in quiet desperation, unfulfilled, unmotivated and unhappy. Such is the life of a "catfish."

These two catfish experiences illustrate one of the tragedies of our times. Think about it. Did anyone ever sit down with you in your youth and give you a formula for determining the personal and career direction that fit you? Most people have never had anyone do that for them.

Discovery

Early on in my career of providing seminars for professionals, business executives and entrepreneurs, I discovered a large number of people who were 10, 15, and 20 plus years into their careers who were still asking themselves the same questions I asked when I was in college: What should I choose as a profession that will enable me to have a successful career and that I would be happy doing?

On any given day, well over 50% of Americans say they are dissatisfied with their work and that they would like to change if they knew what they should be doing or felt they had the freedom to change.

The catfish are everywhere, **but there is a better way!**

In the following chapters you will discover how you as a parent, a mentor or role model for young people can become more aware of negative, unproductive lessons that young people easily learn from their environment that contribute to the catfish catastrophe.

Along with the awareness of these negative lessons are solutions you can put in action that will help the young people in your life:

* Be more self-reliant.
* Be more self-directed.
* Be more self-motivated.
* Develop a great work ethic.
* Make good decisions.
* Resist being swayed by negative peer pressure.
* Set ambitious goals.
* Pick quality friends.
* Discover that there is no "free lunch" in life.
* Expect the best from themselves.
* Value family relationships.
* Have a "make it happen" attitude about life and their future.

It all starts at home. You can be the positive influence in your young person's life – one who will contribute to his or her future personal and professional success.

If you are looking for a way to help the young people in your life save six, seven, ten years or maybe even a lifetime of catfish catastrophe, and instead live happily and successfully today and in the future - read on. It's never too early and never too late to start.

MISTAKE 1
Creating and Fostering the Entitlement Attitude

According to psychologists, narcissistic entitlement is an attitude of "Because I have, I deserve." Some young people develop the belief that whatever socioeconomic level they were raised in is what the world owes them and what the world will give them. To illustrate the lack of maturity represented by this attitude, it is typical of the three-year-old who says to his parents, "It's not fair." When a child uses this expression, it is the first sign of narcissistic entitlement. It is saying that because I exist, I am entitled to certain privileges.

A typical manifestation of this in teen years is the student who says to himself, "My dad is a doctor so I should be accepted into medical school and I should be accepted at a school that is at least as prestigious as the one where he got his training."

I remember a young man who came to Eagle "U" having inherited an unhealthy entitlement attitude from his parents - probably without realizing it. He knew that his grandfather went to Harvard, his dad went to Harvard, and so he had the expectation that he would also go to Harvard. The problem was, however, that he had done nothing to earn that privilege. He felt it was a family entitlement. He wanted the outcome, but his parents had given him no real appreciation for the effort that his father and grandfather had made to obtain what they had achieved. He was due a rude awakening.

The welfare trap often is found within families who have lived on welfare as a way of life, sometimes for generations. Since the parents aren't of a disposition to admit to their children that they are receiving without real entitlement, the children grow up believing the government owes them a handout. They expect to have this subsidy for the rest of their lives.

The children in families that live on government welfare often grow up without ambition, thinking that they will just continue in the same pattern. Others grow up thinking that they are destined to work in jobs that produce minimum wage and don't get a vision of their true potential.

There is a matter of human nature that is a trust officer's nightmare. In most cases when Dad and Mom are alive and well, loving families function with tender consideration for all. However, when both parents pass away and no one who earned the money remains, there is an interesting entitlement ethic that develops as everyone scrambles and sometimes fights for "his share" of the estate. In the opinion of the heirs, the money is just out there and each can think of many reasons why he or she is entitled to a larger share than his or her siblings. It is well to address this problem realistically and not leave it to one's posterity to fight over.

It is out of this entitlement phenomenon that we get the saying "Three generations from shirt-sleeves to shirt-sleeves." The first generation has the major struggle to create a thriving business. The second generation has witnessed the struggle and has an appreciation for what it takes to succeed and at least maintains the status quo. The third generation has seen only the result and not the struggle and too often runs the business into the ground because of the lack of either experience or appreciation for what it took to create the inherited business. Those who don't learn the value of work eventually find their way back to poverty.

Being allowed to just get by in education is another trap. I discovered this one from a relative who worked with students in the intracity schools. In most school systems the revenue the school receives is based on the average number of students who are seated in the classroom during some prescribed period of time. If a student drops out, revenue goes down. The students in intracity schools become aware of the system. They learn that even if they don't study and earn passing grades, there is extreme pressure on the teachers to give them a passing grade so they will stay in the system. Of course those who are not otherwise motivated just loaf along and take advantage of the system. The lack of motivation results in the students' refusing to face the reality that someday they will need to make a living. Some of them just expect to live on the welfare dole as they see their own family and other families doing.

In these schools the parent-teacher conferences usually reveal the root of the problem - the parents are often second generation welfare recipients themselves and have the entitlement ailment.

Fortunately there is a solution for all of this and we will deal with it in the second portion of this chapter.

Driver entitlement is another problem. It is easy to believe the surveys that indicate 99% of students expect to receive a driver's license when they reach age sixteen. The law allows that, so they feel they are entitled to it. There is no sensitivity to the fact that having a license is a privilege that must be earned.

In states that have recognized that 80% of automobile accidents involve those between age sixteen and twenty, a restricted license is issued. It requires new drivers to drive a certain number of hours with a parent or guardian. They are not allowed to have non-family members in the car for six months. They are not allowed to drive at night. In California where these restrictions are enforced, traffic accidents among teenagers have been reduced by 40%.

What about entitlement in the work place? Those who have the entitlement mentality and make it through graduation think they are entitled to a job that puts them in a position up the ladder a little ways with what they consider to be an acceptable salary. They have no concept of the position of the employer who cannot employ them in the long run unless they have a skill and a work ethic that will enable them to produce the revenue that will pay their salaries.

There is another trap where the employer has a requirement that all new employees get a feeling for the work that produces the products the company sells. The new oil company employee might be put to work in a gas station. The plumbing and heating company puts new employees out doing installation and repairs and then into sales training as a requirement for those who want to work into management. Wise managers do this with the MBA graduates as well as the high school graduates. But those who have developed the entitlement complex are sometimes not willing to do what they consider to be menial tasks.

Parents can set up another kind of entitlement trap. Dad owns the business and so the sons or daughters feel they are entitled to begin in management. Wise fathers who have built sound businesses usually don't see it that way.

What do teenagers know about family businesses? When I ask students at Eagle "U" if they know how much their parents make - what the family income is that supports the lifestyle that they have grown up with - it is seldom that 25% have any idea. The next question I ask is how many know what the monthly premium is on the automobile the family owns and that they are allowed to drive. Very few have any idea of the cost and fewer are required to pay a portion of it. I remember one student from California who said he was required to pay part of the extra premium. He said, "It's a killer - $500 a month." Those who have these privileges usually have no idea of these costs. After all, they think they are entitled.

Protecting children from the struggle that the parents experienced is another trap. Parents who have struggled to reach some level of affluence want to see that their children do not have to go through what they went through. As a result, the children not only develop the entitlement complex, but each child insists on receiving the same privileges and/or luxuries that they have seen others receive both in and outside of the family.

The irony of it all is that parents, in bestowing what they think is an expression of love on their children, create just the opposite of what they want their children to have - the motivation and capability to make it on their own.

Do your children have an entitlement attitude? To help you decide, just review these symptoms:

1. Complaining that what they have is not good enough or that their friends have something they don't have.

2. Always wanting to do the fun things and never wanting to do anything that might be considered work.

3. Having the attitude that everything in life should be fun.

4. Insisting on or campaigning for benefits that are totally equal to those received by any or all other siblings and friends.

5. Expecting parents to bail them out of whatever trouble they get into financially or otherwise.

If you identify any of these symptoms, read on. There is a solution.

.

SOLUTION

Maybe you remember the stock brokerage television commercial of a few years ago where the spokesman claimed the firm worked hard to be deserving of customer patronage. With regard to the commissions paid to the company, he said, "We earn it." Parents would do well to have all children develop so that they feel to some degree deserving of the many things provided for them by their parents, grandparents, teachers or anyone else. They need to learn what it takes to be successful when they are on their own. This refers not only to economic success but also the kind of success that focuses on things that will enable them to develop a happy long-lasting lifestyle.

One of the first things that can be done to start younger children off in the right direction is to give them things they are responsible to accomplish on a regular basis. They might be assigned to take out the garbage, clean up a room, help with meal preparation, or help a younger brother or sister. This helps them feel the satisfaction that comes from contributing something to the successful functioning of the family.

An extension of that might be to provide the opportunity for children to earn privileges such as watching TV, playing with a group of friends, going to a birthday party. For instance, it isn't appropriate for the child to go out to play or to a party before his/her room is clean and tidy. There are similar applications of this principle for teenagers. If they want to take the car, they need to leave it clean inside and out. They need to use it responsibly. Their school grades need to be kept at a prescribed level, etc.

Here is a typical entitlement problem that nearly every parent faces. It has to do with the expectation of young people who are old enough to qualify for a driver's license. Many of them also expect to be given a car of their own or at least access to a car. Here's how one father dealt with that problem.

In this instance it was a convenience for the parents to provide a car for their son. The time involved in transporting him to all the places he had to go was excessive. To help the son understand the difference between a right and a privilege, the father created a formal written contract and had his son sign it. It detailed the conditions under which he had the privilege of driving the car. These included getting himself punctually to the places where he was expected to be, getting in at a designated hour after weekend dates, not steady dating any one girl, etc. It was agreeably signed before the son received access to the car.

All went well until the son got serious with a very attractive and somewhat self-centered girl friend. When the successive dates became conspicuous, the dad reminded his son of the contract provision about going steady. He said, "This is what we agreed to and you are in violation of the agreement. So you either have to conform or give me back the keys." The son then had the experience of choosing. It was an agonizing process but as you may guess, he decided to keep the car and give up the girl. Probably both things worked out for the best, including the fact that the son had a good lesson in distinguishing the difference between a right and a privilege. There is a slimmer chance that he discovered that the girl had a lot going for her in terms of appearance but little else.

Here's another problem with cars that needs to be addressed. Affluent parents who have a busy lifestyle need to be sure they don't attempt to make up for neglected time with their children by giving things money will buy - popular brand-name clothes, a car at age sixteen, excessive spending money, etc. Besides the problem that develops from lack of personal attention, there is little sense of responsibility developed in children when they receive luxuries without earning them. A typical example of this occurs when Johnny rolls his expensive car at age 16½. The parents then wonder how he could be so thoughtless. Since the teen has no investment in the luxury of the car, he feels little remorse. Every privilege needs to be earned and teaching that principle is very important.

Sometimes you may get outside help although it isn't wise to depend on that resource. I was privy to an interesting incident in this regard where a teenage boy inadvertently provided a cure for a group of his peers who were suffering from the entitlement syndrome. This happened at an Eagle "U" seminar. The boy in question was the oldest of five children. His mother was working to support the family. His father had passed away at an early age which necessitated the boy's working to help support the family in addition to attending school. He had a first hand knowledge of what it takes to earn a dollar. In the dorms after the day's seminar was over, a group of the students began discussing their various home situations. Some students were griping about the kind of car their parents gave them when they reached driver age and that they didn't get as much for Christmas this year as they did the year before.

After listening to complaints for what must have seemed a long time, the truly underprivileged student stood up and said in effect, "You all make me sick. You are a bunch of spoiled, ungrateful brats. With the attitude you have, I will bet you I will out-earn the whole lot of you combined before I am thirty-five." Thus saying, he went back to his room and left them all with their mouths open.

The next morning when class started, one of the students who was in the room when this outburst occurred, asked if he could say something to the whole class. When permission was granted, he told the class what had happened the night before and said those who had been party to the griping got together after they were scolded. They reviewed their behavior and decided the critical student was right and that they never were going to amount to anything unless they changed their attitudes. The spokesman for the group received a thunderous applause for his confession. As previously stated, parents can't depend on this kind of successful third party intervention, but it's an illustration of the fact that there is a way to teach and gain acceptance of reality.

Here is some guidance on deciding what is a need and what is a want. It would certainly be appropriate to provide college tuition, books, and a meal ticket for a student who has qualified himself for college admittance. After that the earning process might appropriately be having the student earn his/her own money for additional needs, for recreation and other activities. If the career path requires especially heavy courses, the earning might just involve achieving and maintaining grades at a certain level.

In my teen years it was family policy that every boy would qualify as an Eagle Scout before he was allowed to apply for a driver's license. I don't know if my parents would have enforced that policy as an absolute requirement, but I was the last born and none of my three older brothers had dared test the policy so I certainly wasn't going to be the first. Meeting those requirements taught me to follow through and be responsible. This carried over into being a responsible driver.

As an employer now, I watch for Eagle Scout on a resume just like I watch for college graduate. Even more than what skills might be learned in the process of both of these undertakings, the following through that it takes to finish a task, whether it be with school or Eagle Scout requirements, demonstrates the ability and willingness to finish a task once begun. Those who have these credentials most often learned this at an early age and the achievement is just a demonstration of the lesson learned.

Sometimes I interview students at Eagle "U" who are very entrepreneurial minded. They ask why they should finish college. Why not just go out and apply all of their great ideas? They note that Bill Gates didn't finish college so why should they. This is related to some degree to the entitlement mentality. I have to remind them that there is only one Bill Gates in the world and they are better off focusing on the rule rather than the exception. The general rule is that if you finish your education or your Eagle Scout requirements, you will never need to explain why you didn't. If you don't, you'll spend countless hours throughout your life trying to convince people that you are of the nature to follow through on what you start, but as concerns college you didn't think you needed to. This is seldom very convincing.

I helped a shirt-tail relative financially so he could get through college. His mother was an alcoholic and had lived on welfare nearly all of her adult life. I don't know where the young man thought the mother got her money, but he knew that nobody that he ever saw was working to acquire it. By the time he finished college, he had a good understanding of the welfare system and had a mind-set that those who weren't able to make a living would be supported by a big time money dispenser - the U.S. Government or someone else who would happily provide for his needs and in fact also his wants.

On graduation day he announced that he was moving in with us so that he could spend full time studying to take the M-CAT exams and qualify for medical school. He announced that he didn't have time to work. The culture that he grew up in was catching up with him. It was then that I reminded him that he had just devoted four years to acquiring a college education which is something no one in his family had ever done. I complimented him on this achievement. Then I reminded him that the purpose of the four-year degree, which I had helped him to receive, was to give him a credential so he could get a job and make his own way in the world. If he wanted to go to medical school, that was certainly a worthy ambition, but it didn't seem to me that receiving more handouts was an appropriate learning experience for a college graduate.

He became very hostile because he had a mind fix that all those who were successful and had money should share it freely with those who were in need - especially him. What he didn't realize was that his behavior was very typical. Those who receive without paying in some way for what they get, resent those who give it to them. So when the handout is no longer available, the deep down hostility manifests itself because it makes them feel inadequate. This is what was happening.

Forced out on his own, he got a job teaching biology in a low income central city high school. After a year of that, he came back saying that this was the most valuable experience of his life. He had seen how the other half lives and realized how valuable the lessons he had learned were. He now had an idea of what it takes to make a living just to sustain himself. That was at least a start on the road to a successful life.

Admittedly it is very difficult for parents or anyone else to decide what is generous and thoughtful and what at the same time will help a prospective recipient to learn an important lesson that lasts a lifetime. The temptation for parents is to take the path of least resistance and fix the problem with money, influence or whatever else satisfies their need to feel that they have fulfilled their parental obligations. The difficult thing is to do what is needed. The best course of action is often the most painful.

Thinking ahead. I learned this lesson from a multi-millionaire of my acquaintance who had built a very large jewelry manufacturing business that had distribution throughout the country. On the occasion of note, he had a video made that was to be shown only after he passed away. In it he greeted his family warmly, and then said that in his will he had provided for each member of the family in the manner that he thought appropriate. He then admonished them to keep in mind that none who were to be recipients had done anything to earn the things they were receiving. This was a very forceful reminder that the inheritance was a gift not an entitlement.

He said that his company properly belonged to those who had worked with him to build it, and that if any of his family attempted to acquire additional inheritance arising out of the value of the company, they would be cut off totally from receiving even the things he had provided for them. It was a great piece of literature and I would have liked to have been in the room when it was shown. He was a very wise father.

A second and very important part of the entitlement problem has to do with teaching children that they must live with the consequences of the things they choose to do.

Here's an example of allowing children to learn from the consequences of their actions. Two young men were working together on a project in a small town in the central part of North Carolina many miles away from their homes. In their work they befriended a repairman who worked for the local telephone company. One day, the man revealed to them a phone number that could be used to circumvent the local phone exchange and connect them with the long distance lines without a toll charge. That night they went to a phone booth in a rather obscure place in the city and began calling friends all over the country. As the time got late they became more and more fascinated with this new found free telephoning system.

During the evening the police drove by several times and noted the boys in the phone booth hour after hour. They eventually checked with the local phone exchange to see where the boys were calling. When there was no record of the calls, the boys were picked up and jailed for defrauding the phone company. Since it was in interstate commerce, the crime was a felony.

When the boys' supervisor got into it, he called their parents. The mother responded when the call went to the first set of parents. She immediately voiced her concern that her son might lose his job and that her neighbors might find out that her son had been put in jail. She was anxious to know how she could get him out of the situation before all this got into the local papers.

The call to the second boy's parents was quite different. The father answered the phone. His first reaction was, "Harry knows that if he has done something wrong, he will have to pay for it." Interestingly enough it was the first boy who had initiated the idea of using the information they had gleaned from the telephone company employee. He talked the second boy into participating. He was no doubt brought up in a home where there was always someone there to bail him out of whatever trouble he got into. He was still expecting it. He hadn't yet learned that everything must be earned and that for every act there is a consequence - in this instance jail time and a fine.

So all this gets back to the two lessons parents need to teach to prevent their children from developing the entitlement attitude:

1. Teach them to do it the old fashioned way - to earn it. Teach that they must do what is required in order to get whatever it is they want. It doesn't just show up.

2. Teach that there is a consequence to every action - good or bad - and that what you sow, so shall you reap.

MISTAKE 2
Failing to Develop a Proper Deserve Level

Entitlement and deserve. There is a difference. It might be helpful to make a clear distinction between the two. To do so let's start with Merriam Webster in the E's and D's.

Entitlement is "to give a person a just claim."

Deserve is "to show by conduct or qualities to be worthy of reward, rightfully merited or earned."

It is the removing of the "rightfully merited and earned" requirement that is the difference between the two terms. It is always giving to young people without their having earned it that creates the entitlement trap. Likewise, it is the doing for young people instead of allowing them to do for themselves that creates a low deserve level in them.

Providing Too Much Help

We seem to be born with an innate knowledge and desire to be independent and self-reliant. I have been reminded of this each time one of our children reaches the age when she can communicate.

It usually happens when the family is in a hurry to get somewhere and I am trying to move things along. In an effort to speed up the process, I will be helping one of the younger children get dressed, something she is very capable of doing on her own. Her reaction is usually, "Daddy, I can do it myself!"

What we may consider an expression of love is not always a wise service. In an effort to show love to children, it is a common mistake to do for them what they can do for themselves. While a certain amount of service teaches courtesy and consideration, we find many young people's deserve level has been crippled by parents who do too much for them so that they don't have confidence in their own capability. They then get into the habit of waiting for someone else to do things for them.

It starts early in life. Each incident of doing something for a child may not be significant in itself, but the cumulative effect can be devastating. As a parent, take the following short quiz and see how many of these things you have been guilty of doing for your children in the past. Most have to do with things we do or did for children when they were very young--ages three to six. It is an indication of the message we have sent to them at an early age about their ability to do things for themselves.

On a regular basis do you do any of the following for your young children?

Yes	No	
□	□	Clean their rooms or pick up after them.
□	□	Hire help to clean their rooms or pick up after them.
□	□	Get up from the dinner table to get something they want after everyone has begun the meal.
□	□	Help them get dressed when they already know how.
□	□	Get them a drink of water at their request.
□	□	Make their sack lunch to take to school when they could do it themselves.

☐ ☐   Place their order for them when eating at a restaurant.

☐ ☐   Be spokesman for them with another adult when they have a special request.

☐ ☐   Put their clean clothes away for them.

☐ ☐   Talk on their behalf to adults instead of letting them talk for themselves.

Doing any one of these things is no big deal. But the combined effect over time of doing two or more of them repeatedly sends the quiet but powerful underlying message: **"I have to do this for you because I don't think you can do if for yourself."**

It erodes your children's deserve level--slowly.

Low deserve level on the inside will eventually show up as low achievement on the outside. To demonstrate how prevalent the low deserve level problem is and its eventual consequences, we do an exercise with the young people we work with at Eagle "U" that makes this concept come alive.

The mass in the middle. A group of twenty-five to thirty students who have been together for a day or two are given the assignment to organize themselves in a straight line in order of where they think they will probably be on the ladder of success in comparison with the others in the group twenty years in the future. The exercise is for each to negotiate a position in the group. As they proceed, there are usually two or three who jockey for position at the head of the line, picturing themselves as the most successful in the group. The majority, however, seek a place somewhere comfortably in the middle. Those who choose to be at the top are few.

When the group is asked why there was so little negotiating for the top spot, there is always a deserve level issue involved. Most say there are others who are smarter, more skilled, or who can do things better than they can. They believe those other people deserve the top spot.

The heart of the deserve level is the belief in one's personal ability to achieve a level of success--however success is defined for that particular area of life. If you haven't had a lot of experience with working, doing, and accomplishing, then it is easy to believe that you can't do it. So you will rarely even make the attempt. You'll just stay in the mediocre middle where it's comfortable.

Crippling by Comparison

You are what you think you are. I was talking with a group of college students at Eagle "U" one day. In the group was a very spirited, super-attractive 21 year-old female college student. While questioning her about things she had thought about for a career, I received a recitation of a long list of things she was not good at or could not do. She said, "I'm not a very good people person. I'm not good at math, etc. etc." She was very well versed in things she thought she was not capable of doing.

I finally asked her who had filled her with all of that negativism. She said, "What do you mean?" My reply was, "At a very young age you have figured out a lot of things you can't do. Who taught you that?" She just got a quizzical look on her face. I told her that at her age she was not likely to have had enough experience to know so much about what she could and could not do. She didn't realize it but she was very down on herself. What she thought she deserved or was capable of accomplishing was way down in the basement level.

It is human nature to compare ourselves with others. Unhealthy, but natural. It becomes toxically damaging to our deserve level when we start comparing our weaknesses to someone else's strengths.

Kindergarten vs. college. The next time you are with children who are around the age of five, try this little exercise. Ask them if they can play the piano, dance, sing, draw a pretty picture, etc. You name it, they will say they can do it.

Next, take that same list of things to college-age students. Most often they will identify very few things on the list they can do, and they will produce a long list of reasons why they are not very good at doing even the few things they identify.

What's going on here? The fact is that a college student can more than likely do every one of those things better than the kindergartner. The difference is in how each interprets the question. The kindergartner hears, "Can you do this?" "Do you have the ability or willingness to try it?" The college-age person hears, "Are you good at it?" "How do you compare with everyone else in these areas?"

A healthy deserve level comes from the belief that you are capable of earning, accomplishing or doing what you set your mind to. A low deserve level comes from only seeing what others have done and comparing it to what you have never really worked at. And then believing that that is just the way it is.

Often, we make those unhealthy comparisons ourselves. It gets worse when those comparisons are made for us by an authority figure--parent, teacher, advisor, coach, and others.

Why can't you? This question became painfully clear to me in the fifth grade. One of my best friends was a boy whom we'll call Ted. He was the youngest in a family of high achievers. All of his older siblings had distinguished themselves in various ways. One was high school student body president, another was quarterback of the high school football team, etc. Since Ted was much younger than his brothers, they had a big head start in life and I'm sure he naturally felt as if he had a lot to live up to.

It was only made worse the day our fifth grade teacher, who had taught one of Ted's older brothers, was attempting to get some degree of discipline in the class. Ted happened to be in the middle of some of the chaos. In an effort to gain control she said to him, "Why can't you be like your brother?" The impact was immediate. You could see the disappointment on his face. It was obvious that she had verbalized the question he had on his mind almost every day. The comparison was devastating.

Lowering Your Children's Sense of Self-worth without Realizing It

One of the most revealing deserve level exercises we conduct at Eagle "U" involves assembling a group of mentors (successful people from many fields of endeavor) and giving the students an opportunity to talk to them, to get their advice and gain from their experience. Each student can choose the fields he or she is interested in and then is afforded the opportunity to sit down with successful people in those fields one-on-one. It provides a great opportunity for them to get sound advice and make some valuable connections.

Invariably a large number of the students ask why these very successful and busy people would be willing to take time out to talk to someone who is just a student. These comments are a reflection of their deserve level. In some way, they feel they are not worthy or deserving of taking the time of such successful busy people.

Many times the messages from parents to children that are meant to keep things under control make an impression that carries over into young adult and adult life. Messages such as:

> "Don't bother the nice man."
> "He is way too busy to talk to you."
> "Please stay out of the way."
> "Be quiet."
> "Don't speak until you are spoken to."
> "Don't interrupt."

And then there is the almighty "No, No, No, No, No." Most children are told "No!" so many times by age eight that it is a wonder they don't think their name is No No! All these admonitions carry a subtle message that "You, my child, are a nuisance or at least a bother and don't deserve whatever it is you want." It is unfortunately a lot easier, or at least more convenient at any given time, to stop the behavior than to provide a positive alternative.

In the extreme, these messages can lead young people to believe that they are hardly worthy enough to occupy space in the world, not to mention going out and asking for things they want.

Is Your Young Person's Deserve Level Under Attack?

❑ What things do you do for the young people in your life that they are capable of doing for themselves?

❑ Do they compare their weaknesses to others' strengths?

❑ Do you or other authority figures ever compare them with other siblings, friends, or peers?

❑ How many "stay out of the way" messages have they internalized to an extreme?

SOLUTION
Build a Healthy Deserve Level

Building a healthy deserve level can start at an early age. We've observed through our work with young people that, like most things in life, some seem to naturally develop a higher deserve level than others. In any case, here are some simple things that would be healthy for all young people to experience that would help them to build the belief that they deserve, or they are capable of accomplishing, what they set out to accomplish in life.

Creating every day opportunities to do things for themselves. Several years ago I was invited to speak to a group of high school juniors and seniors in upstate New York. The family who had extended the invitation invited me to be their houseguest. After dinner the first night, the three teen and preteen children were in a flurry of activity. One was clearing the table, the other washing the dishes and the youngest child, Joel, age nine, was busy working the phones organizing the weekly carpool driving assignments for his 5:30 a.m. hockey practice. He was the organizer who was doing all of the work--not Mom nor Dad.

When I inquired about what was going on, Joel's response was very matter of fact. He said, "I want to play hockey. Practice is held every weekday morning at 5:30 a.m. Mom and Dad have agreed to take me two days a week and I have to make arrangements to get there the other three days."

To him, what he was doing at age nine was no big deal. But I could not help but compare what most of his peers would be experiencing at his age in a similar situation--Mom or Dad would be on the phone doing it for them.

Joel's parents had this basic core philosophy: **Never do for young people what they are capable of doing for themselves.**

As a result of his doing something for himself that he was very capable of doing, he was learning skills and character traits that would serve him well for a lifetime: organization, responsibility, dependability, communication, and taking initiative, just to name a few.

Constructive and destructive help. I accompanied my six year-old daughter to one of her first piano lessons. As she sat down at the piano, her teacher asked her in a reminding tone if the bench was in the proper position. Now I try diligently to treat our daughters with courtesy, for one thing so that when they are of dating age they will gravitate to boys who are similarly courteous and helpful--those raised as gentlemen. So in that spirit, I jumped to my feet heading for the bench. The teacher seeing my intent asked me courteously to sit back down. She explained that one of the things our daughter had been taught was that before she sits down at the piano she is to put the bench in a position that will enable her to play properly. She pointed out that since I would not likely be on hand every time she played the piano, I should not do for her what she can and must remember to do for herself.

Reflecting on this I became aware of how easy it is to make this mistake with the very best of intentions. Our daughter moved the bench. She did it just fine, but it would have made me feel very fatherly to do it for her.

There are literally hundreds of ways we may want to help our children and some are probably very acceptable. However, those things that require experience and to which there is advantage for them to do for themselves, they should have the experience of doing.

Now imagine how I felt when I attended Ashlin's first piano recital a few weeks later. When it was her turn on the program, she walked to the front of the room and the first thing she checked was the bench position. The look of confidence she had, knowing just what to do and how to do it, confirmed the wisdom of the teacher, and the lesson was emphasized again for her father!

Replace "Let me help you" with "Will you help me?" In the business and professional seminars we conduct through our company, there is a customer service principle we teach that says: **People like themselves better when they are helping you than when you are helping them.**

While we all enjoy receiving great customer service wherever we go, it is a great self-esteem builder whenever someone asks for our help. It fulfills the desire we have to be of worth to others. Imagine the underlying message to young people when someone whom they perceive as older, wiser, and very capable, asks for their help. It sends the message, "I see you as a very able person who is capable of doing things that are of value to me."

The "Can you help me?" message is as powerful in a positive way as the "Let me help you" message can be in a negative and destructive way.

The "I can do it" attitude. When our oldest daughter was only about three, I asked her to help me bring in the empty garbage container from the street curb after the garbage pick-up. I asked her to take hold of the handle as we wheeled the container up the long steep driveway to the house. Midway in our journey I commented to her that I thought she could probably do it herself, and so I carefully let go of the handle. She took over and successfully pulled the container the rest of the way up the hill. When we got to the top, she stopped, turned around, looked down the hill she had just conquered and exclaimed, "I can do it, Daddy, I can do it!"

The heart of a healthy deserve level is the "I can do it" attitude. It is the belief that you are capable of accomplishing what you set out to do.

It takes time. I'm always impressed with the young teenagers who come to the first level of Eagle "U" who fill out their own paperwork, make their own flight arrangements and communicate everything to us themselves. In most cases, it would be faster, easier, and less hassle for their parents to do it. Every first experience takes time, patience, and some training. But every little opportunity can be a deserve level building experience. In the same light, I get concerned when the college students we work with at Eagle "U" still have parents who are doing all of these things for them--things they can and should be doing for themselves.

Remember: **Love is not doing things for your children, it is letting them do things for themselves.**

When they do, they learn, grow, become self-reliant, and internalize the belief that they are capable of accomplishing things they set out to do.

Avoiding the Comparison Trap

The fable of the animal school. It was Dr. George H. Reavis who put his imagination to work on the subject of comparing our weaknesses to others' natural abilities in his fable of the animal school. Here is a brief version of his story:

The animals got together and decided they must do something heroic to meet the problems of the great new world. So they organized a school. They adopted an activity curriculum consisting of running, climbing, swimming and flying. To make it easier to administer, as we do in our public schools, all of the animals took the same courses and were graded based on their comparative performance.

The duck was excellent in swimming, better in fact than the instructor. He made passing grades in flying, but was very poor in running, especially compared to the rabbit. Since he was slow in running, he had to stay after school and also drop swimming to practice running. This kept up until his webbed feet were badly worn and that made him only average in swimming. But average was acceptable in the school so nobody worried about it except the duck.

The rabbit started at the top of the class in running, but had a nervous breakdown because of so much make-up work in swimming.

The squirrel was excellent in climbing, but developed frustration in the flying class. His teacher made him start from the ground up instead of from the treetop down. The squirrel also developed a charley horse from over exertion and as a consequence got a "C" in climbing and a "D" in running.

The eagle was a major problem and was severely disciplined. In the climbing class he beat all the others to the top of the tree, but insisted on using his own way to get there.

At the end of the year of training, an abnormal eel that could swim exceedingly well, run, climb, and fly a little, had the highest average and was valedictorian. When it came time for graduation, most of the others were still involved in make-up work in those things where they lacked proficiency.

Ridiculous? Not really. It is the reality that most of us experienced in school. We just don't measure up as the best in every area compared to the best in each area.

One of the greatest gifts young people can receive is the understanding that they have particular things at which they are naturally talented and gifted. Instead of comparing their greatest weakness to other people's strengths, they need to identify where their strengths are and build on them.

Everyone has strengths. Our belief at Eagle "U" is that all people have something they are more gifted in than at least 10,000 other people. I did not always think that applied to me, however. Going into my senior year in high school, my very insightful father helped me gain a new perspective on where my strengths were. He took me and one of my older brothers to the Johnson O'Connor Research Foundation Human Engineering Lab, an eighty plus year-old organization dedicated to helping people understand their natural aptitudes.

After nearly two days of testing, each of us was presented with an analysis of our aptitudes compared to those of thousands of other people who had been tested over the previous decades. All the grading was done on charts and graphs so we could see exactly how we compared to the rest of the world, at least the rest of the world they had tested.

When I opened the grading folder and looked at the results of my tests, I was shocked. There was not a single talent line on my graph that went above the fiftieth percentile.

I was average or below in everything. Just before I was ready to sink into a lifetime depression over the realization that just about everyone was better than I was in every area of life, the counselor started my analysis by saying, "You have the perfect profile for a manager. You have average skills in nearly everything, but no excesses."

The analyst told me I would never be distracted from concentrating on management responsibilities by wanting to do a particular task that someone else could do just as well. I would be willing to delegate. It turned out to be a very deserve level building experience. I realized that having no talents in excess was my greatest strength. From that moment on, it didn't bother me to discover that someone else had a talent superior to mine.

Despite the message that is easy to pick up in school--that you are supposed to be great at everything--one of the greatest gifts young people can receive is an understanding of their natural gifts and talents so they can build on them. Their deserve level will be higher and their success and fulfillment will be much greater in the future.

Use Verbal Skills
That Will Raise Your Children's Deserve Level

The messages we receive beginning in the earliest days of childhood have a dramatic impact on our deserve level. I'd like to suggest some minor verbal skill surgery in just a few areas that can make a major difference in the lives of the children and teenagers in your life.

Deserve Level Verbal Skill #1: Teach your children how to interrupt in an acceptable way. The "Don't interrupt me" message can communicate, "You're not important or deserving of my attention." While everyone needs to learn sooner or later the socially correct way to wait his/her turn, I'm amazed that most people have a real hang-up here. Either they were so severely reprimanded as children for interrupting that in adulthood they won't ask anyone for anything, or they never learned the lesson and they dominate every conversation.

We have some friends who have done a beautiful job of developing a system with their children for interrupting in an acceptable way. If Mom or Dad is talking on the phone or is in the middle of a conversation with someone face to face, the children know they can quietly go up and just touch Mom or Dad on the arm or hand. That is their mutually agreed upon signal that something is needed. The parents are on notice and the child knows that attention will come as soon as possible. It sends the message, "You are important and I'll get to you as soon as I can." For older children, a similar system might be developed.

Deserve Level Verbal Skill #2: Focus on what you want your children to do, not on what you don't want them to do. We are bombarded with so many "No" messages in childhood that it is a miracle that we emerge psychologically sound. Except for extreme cases where life or death and safety are involved, the "No" approach is not psychologically sound in itself.

You cannot focus on the opposite of an idea. You just can't. If I were to tell you, "Don't think of the Statue of Liberty," you wouldn't be able to get its image out of your mind. What about "Don't think about elephants?" The first thing that comes to mind is that big gray animal with a long trunk and large floppy ears, the very thing I don't want you to think about.

Similarly, the moment you say, "Don't talk," "Don't touch," "Don't run," "Don't pick your nose!" "Don't spend so much time on the phone," "Don't stay out too late," the very thing you don't want your child to do is the very thing that sticks in his or her mind.

Instead of requesting what you don't want, stay focused on what you do want. For example:

> "Will you quietly wait here until I am finished?"
> "Will you just look at the pretty things?"
> "Can you please walk so you'll be safe?"
> "Can you keep your hands away from your face?"
> "Will you please finish up your phone conversations with your friends in ten minutes?"
> "You need to be home before midnight. Will you be here?"

The baseball coach who always says to a player just as he is going to bat, "Don't strike out," can count on a dramatic decrease in that player's batting average. All the player can think about is striking out.

The good baseball coach who wants a winning team always says "Hit the ball!" right before the player goes to bat. As the player approaches the plate, what he thinks about is just that, hitting the ball.

If you want a winning young person, be like the winning baseball coach. Keep the focus on what you want, not on what you don't want. You'll often get it!

Deserve Level Verbal Skill #3:   Replace "No" with an alternative choice. Nobody likes to be rejected, nobody. Have you ever found yourself in a battle of the wills between you and your children when they want to do something that is not appropriate at the time? It usually sounds like this:

They say:	You say:
"I don't want to go to bed."	"Yes you do, right now!"
"Can I go out and play?"	"Not right now."
"Can Jimmy come over?"	"Maybe later."
"Can I take the car?"	"NO!"
"Can I go out with my friends?"	"Not tonight."

Outright rejection, especially without a stated reason, only creates resentment and more of the behavior we don't want. It only creates a feeling of powerlessness to do anything at all which has a negative effect on a healthy deserve level.

So here's a simple solution. Try giving alternatives instead of rejection. For example:

Child says:
"I don't want to go to bed."
You might say:
"I know you don't. Would you rather get ready for bed now or have five more minutes to play?"

Child says:
"Can I go out to play?"
You say:
"We're just about ready to sit down for dinner. Would you like to play outside for twenty minutes after dinner or wait until morning?"

Child says:
"Can Jimmy come over?"
You say:
"You remember our rule that no friends come over until your homework is finished. Would you like to finish your homework now and see if there is time left to have Jimmy come over, or would you rather just wait until tomorrow to have him come?"

Teenager says:
"Can I take the car?"
You say:
"Mom needs the car to go to her hair appointment. Would you like to make arrangements with one of your friends for a ride or plan ahead for another time to use the car?"

Teenager says:
"Can I go out with my friends tonight?"

You say:

"We really need your help to stay with your little brother tonight. Would you like to invite one of your friends over, or would you rather plan for another evening to go out with them?"

Will this always work? No! It is nearly impossible to find something that works one hundred percent of the time. But if your intent is good, your results with these verbal skills will be much better than just outright rejection, and the long-term effect on your young person's deserve level will be much better as well.

Deserve Level Verbal Skill #4: Encourage them to do things for themselves even when they ask you to do them. This one is tricky and is the reason parents spend hours doing things for their children that their children are very capable of doing and would benefit from doing for themselves.

It starts at an early age at the dinner table. After everyone is seated for the meal, little Johnny says, "Mommy, can you get me a drink of water?" Mom then jumps up to fulfill the request. Just when she settles in again, Johnny says, "Mommy, can I have some catsup?" Up she goes again. And so the entire meal goes. It finally ends with Johnny going off to play leaving his dirty dishes on the table for someone else to clean up.

Keeping in mind our earlier principle that love is not "doing for" but letting them "do for themselves," consider answering your children's questions or requests with a question in return, and then directing them in a way that will allow them to do what they are capable of doing. As a side benefit, it will free up a tremendous amount of your time.

Child says:
"Can you get me a drink of water?"
You say:
"Would you like a drink of water? Great! You're welcome to hop down from the table and get one."

Note: Make sure to set up the system so that cups for little kids are stored in the kitchen at little kid level and that they have a stool to reach the water faucet. Make it easy for them to do for themselves around the house.

Child says:
"Will you make me a lunch for tomorrow?"
You say:
"It sounds like you want to take your lunch instead of buying it. Am I right? Great! There is some bread and deli meat in the refrigerator along with some fresh fruit. You are welcome to make your sandwich and grab the fruit of your choice for your lunch tomorrow."

Pre-teen says:
"Can you iron my shirt for the birthday party this afternoon?"
You say:
"You want to look good for the party, don't you? The ironing board is setup in the laundry room. If you will just turn on the iron and wait for about two minutes for it to warm up, you are welcome to get started on it right now!"

Too many young people are crippled by parents who do simple things for them that they are very capable of doing. So practice answering their questions and requests with a question and then suggesting how to do the task themselves.

If you love them, let them do it for themselves. They will learn that they can do it. Their deserve level will go up. They will love you for it—eventually.

Deserve Level Verbal Skill #5: Quit making requests. Get a commitment. Do you ever get sick and tired of barking out orders around the house that don't get obeyed?

"How many times do I have to tell you to pick up your room?"

"This is the third time I've asked you to take out the garbage."

"Can't anyone besides me put these dishes in the dishwasher?"

Commands or requests are just that, commands and requests. They are not often taken seriously. But allowing unfulfilled requests does serious damage to one's deserve level. If someone has asked you to do something and you don't do it, you eventually start feeling diminished because deep down inside you know you are not doing what you ought to do.

Lesson learned from a chef. Gordon Sinclair, the famous Chicago restaurateur, had a serious problem with no-shows. Over thirty percent of patrons who made reservations did not show up. His reservationist, with good intent, would courteously request, "If you have a conflict that will keep you from honoring your reservation, please give us a call." Nothing changed and the thirty percent no-shows continued.

Mr. Sinclair then suggested that his reservationist change just two words in her dialogue. Those two words dramatically reduced no-shows from over thirty percent down to ten percent. What were the two words? **"Will you...."**

"Mr. Jones, if you have any kind of conflict that will prevent you from honoring your reservation, **will you** please call us?" She would then wait for the customer to make a verbal commitment.

What was wrong in this restaurant is the same thing that is wrong in home kitchens everywhere. Too many requests, not enough commitments. Start asking for commitments from your children:

"Johnny, **will you** please go and clean your room right now?"

"Beth, **will you** take out the garbage right now?"

"Sid, **will you** please clean up the dishes tonight before you leave the kitchen?"

Always make sure you get the verbal commitment after you ask for it.

The deserve level gets a boost every time people do what they say they will do. To be the person you desire to be is natural human desire. Requests don't tap into that desire. Asking for a commitment does.

Ask your young people for lots of commitments. Follow up to make sure they follow through, and you'll watch their deserve level soar. **Will you do it?**

Deserve Level Action Plan

1. Let your young people do more for themselves. In fact don't do anything for them that they are or should be capable of doing for themselves. The more they do, the stronger their deserve level will be.

2. Help them identify their strengths. Avoid comparing their weaknesses to someone else's best talents. All people have something they can do better than ten thousand other people. Help them find it and watch their deserve level rise.

3. Watch your tongue! Use good "deserve level verbal skills."

* Teach your children how to interrupt courteously.

* Tell them what to do instead of what not to do.

* Give them a choice instead of saying "No."

* Answer their requests with a question. Encourage them to do things for themselves even when they ask you to do them.

* Ask for commitments; don't make requests. **Will you?**

MISTAKE 3
Failing to Recognize That Your Children Will Not Likely Rise Above What You Expect of Them

An interesting thing about life--people don't often rise above what is expected of them.

About expectation. One of our daughters waited with great anticipation for the arrival of her first day of kindergarten. She couldn't wait to climb on the school bus and experience an expanded world.

The weeks and months that followed after school started, however, brought a disturbing change in her attitude and her behavior. Many days I would wait with great anticipation to hear about her exciting day at school. I would stand at the front door as the school bus pulled up and she got off. But over time, our once enthusiastic child became less and less energetic. She would slowly get off the bus and walk to the house. Our inquiries about her day were met with one and two word answers. Each day getting ready for school in the morning became more and more of a major project that included tears, frustration and over obsession with details.

Then the notes started coming from her teacher saying she was worried about our daughter's behavior in school. She didn't seem to be interacting with the other children and was keeping to herself. The teacher reflected concern because she didn't seem to be developing socially. We passed the whole thing off as symptoms of just getting settled into a new routine. We thought she would get over it and things would return to normal.

Finally, after several more notes from school and a discussion with her teacher, I found a quiet moment with our daughter one evening when the communication channels were wide open and she seemed to be willing to talk at a meaningful level.

I openly shared her teacher's concerns and asked our daughter to share her feelings with me about what was going on. Her response was unexpected and disturbing.

She said that the teacher yelled a lot at the kids who were misbehaving. So for fear of being caught in the line of fire, she chose to lay low, stay out of the way, and try to go unnoticed. Most of the time she would just hold her ground and not participate in order to protect herself. Because many in the class were treated as problems, the entire class rose to the occasion and became exactly what was expected of them-- problem children in one way or another.

When you treat children as problems, they most often meet your expectations!

Sow today and reap tomorrow. One of our chores as children was to help tend the family garden. Each spring we would till the ground, dig the furrows and help plant the seeds. On a regular basis we would have to weed, water and care for the plants as they grew and finally produced vegetables. Each year in late summer and early fall as we harvested the vegetables, a very valuable lesson of nature was reinforced: **In life, you reap what you sow.**

The laws that govern the garden also rule the fertile soil of the mind, heart, attitudes and emotions of very young children. Ages zero to six and on up to eight are the fertile sowing years. How children are treated, especially by their parents and primary caregivers in those impressionable years, determines what their attitudes and personalities will be like in the years to come.

Children who are yelled at, treated with disrespect, and talked down to will not only respond with bad behavior, but all of the behaviors that they have learned by example will eventually grow, develop, and come into full bloom when they become teenagers.

Treat them as problems today and they will continue to be a problem today. They will also retain a memory of the way they were treated and echo it back to you when they get a little older and get their courage up.

The Negative Effect of Overhear Psychology

The principle of overhear psychology says: **That which is overheard makes a deeper impression on listeners than that which is spoken to them directly.**

My best friend and I were on our way home from elementary school one Friday afternoon with great anticipation of a long holiday weekend ahead. We talked about all of the fun things we were going to do. As we walked in the front door of his home, his mother was seated on the couch talking with a friend on the phone. I have never forgotten what she said to her friend as we arrived. "Well, the boys are home. This is going to be a loooooooooong weekend around here for me, I'll tell you that. Having to deal with these children for three solid days is going to drive me crazy."

What we overheard her say was more powerful than anything she could have ever said to us directly. We knew immediately what she was expecting of us and we were happy to accommodate!!! Consciously or subconsciously, we made it a a veeeeeeery long weekend for her. And I suspect we did drive her crazy!

You create low expectations for young people by talking to others about the behavior you don't like.

When I was a young teenager, our family went on a picnic with a distant relative and his family. Our families had children who were about the same ages. During dinner, the adults who were sitting at one end of the picnic table were having a typical adult conversation while the children were chowing down on hamburgers at the other end of the table. Since all we were doing was eating, it was very easy to overhear what the adults were talking about.

All during dinner the other parents were telling my mom and dad about the trials and troubles their fourteen year-old teenager was giving them. They said things such as, "She won't talk to us." "She is defiant." "We can't get her to do anything we ask her to do." And so the list of grievances went on, all within earshot of the their daughter who was eating with us at the other end of the table.

I couldn't help thinking even at my young age that this was not very smart on the part of her parents. It was obvious she could hear everything they were saying and apparently they knew it. All they were doing was communicating their low expectations of her and her behavior. The more they described her bad behavior, the more she felt as if she had license or even obligation to do the things they described. She couldn't help but follow through and live up to the image her parents were creating of her.

When mentors fail in their role. One of the principles we espouse at Eagle "U" is the power of having mentors. I stress to the students how much their parents really want to see them succeed and would give them some great advice and direction if they, the student, would just ASK and LISTEN! Usually the parents are amazed when the young person initiates and asks for a mentor relationship and the young people are surprised at how much their parents really know that can help them!

Several years ago, a seventeen year-old young man approached me after a session in which I had encouraged the students to ask their parents to be their mentor. "I can't do it. In fact, I won't do it." He was upset and disturbed. As we talked, he told me that he did not trust his parents. Every time he shared a problem that he needed help with, it always seemed to leak out. Within days of sharing a challenge or a problem with them it seemed that a sibling, close friend of the family, or even a neighbor would make some offhand comment such as, "How is your chemistry grade coming?" or "Too bad your girlfriend dumped you."

It was obvious to him that his parents--one or both--were

talking about his problems and their disappointments in him to others inside and outside of the family. It was humiliating and demoralizing for him.

Labels We Give Children
Communicate Expectations

Remember the classic childhood defense when someone called you a mean name on the playground–"Sticks and stones may break my bones, but names will never hurt me!"

Nice defense at the moment, but the truth is exactly the opposite. The names as labels we put on children and young people communicate the expectation we have regarding their behavior. These labels stick as tightly as the ones on a glass jar of pickles.

I cringe every time I observe a parent attempting to control the behavior of a misbehaving child by saying things such as:

* "I told you to put that back. You never listen!"

* "How did it break? You're always so careless."

* "There you go again, always doing the wrong thing at the wrong time."

* "You are so slow. Can't you ever be ready on time?"

* "You are always getting into trouble."

* "You're so clumsy. Don't you ever watch where you are going?"

Phrases like these only reinforce the behavior you don't want by telling the young person who and what you think they are. The expectations being so clearly communicated will often be realized.

So the next time you are tempted to use a negative label or

name, just remember that jar of pickles. It is a lot easier to put the label on than it is to take it off. So be very careful what label goes on in the first place!

It might also be well to remember in relations with children (as well as with your spouse or those you work with) that using the word "always" when making an accusation creates tension and frustration. It means "all the time" and since that is non-specific–always wrong, always slow, always late–it's not likely true and also is indefensible. That's why it just creates friction and frustration as well as low expectation.

Are You Setting Expectations Too Low?

Are you guilty of creating low expectations in any of these areas?

- ❑ How do you or did you treat your children ages zero to eight? How you treat them at this age may very well be the way they treat you when they become teenagers!

- ❑ Do you yell, talk down to or treat your young people with disrespect when they "act up?"

- ❑ Are you ever guilty of saying negative things about your children when they are within ear-shot so they overhear?

- ❑ Do you ever talk about your children in negative terms to others--even when your children are not around?

- ❑ What labels or names have you placed on your young people as a result of their perceived bad behavior by saying something like, "Why are you so thoughtless?"

SOLUTION
Expect the Best and You Will Likely Get It!

The visit from one of the leaders of the local church we attended in a city where we lived some years ago signaled the need for help. After he sat down, he asked if my wife, Cheryl, would accept the responsibility to teach a Sunday School class of five and six year-old children. "Before you accept," he said, "please know that this class has gone through a number of teachers recently. The boys are a real handful." In a nearly apologetic tone he said, "We really appreciate your willingness to do this."

The boys in question had gained quite the reputation at a young age. They were often discussed among the parents because of their behavior. Because of their reputation they were often treated as behavior problems, and so they lived up to that expectation.

I watched in amazement the outcome of Cheryl's first class with this young group. She started out by communicating with them with love and respect, and then asked them what type of behavior they thought was appropriate in a good class. She wrote their answers on the board. She asked them what they would like about such a well-behaved class. With their help, she set up a system of appropriate awards and punishments for their new behavior code. They each then gave her permission to enforce the rules they had all decided on based on the rewards and punishments they had created. Since it was their idea, she was never the so-called "bad guy." She was just doing what they had all agreed on previously. They all agreed to help regulate the behavior of class members as well.

Week after week she treated them like little adults. They responded by raising their hands before talking and being polite to each other. At the end of the year, they all came over to our house for a fun party. Their behavior was impeccable.

As a result of this whole process, they liked themselves better because they behaved better. And they loved their teacher because she expected the very best from them and they rose to that expectation.

Fast forward ten years. Imagine inviting a group of a hundred or so teenagers to your house for three or four days. If that image strikes fear in your heart and visions of chaos and disorder, I wouldn't blame you.

At our high school session of Eagle "U," we have students attend from many different backgrounds, different parts of the country, and many who don't really think being there is a good idea, mostly because their parents thought it would be! I am always amazed at how the behavior of each class always rises to the expectations we create in that environment. We start by expecting professionalism, adult behavior, and positive attitude. We treat them the same way. Inevitably we get model behavior from each group. They like themselves better when they have high expectations to live up to, and they start expecting it of their peers around them as well. We are totally convinced that:

If you want positive behavior, you must start with positive expectations.

The Power of Positive Overhear Psychology

Early in my childhood I developed an obsession with building things, often with Legos®. I would spend hours after school playing on the family room floor building some great original creation I had dreamed up. Since the family room was just off of the kitchen, I was always within earshot of my mother when she was busy fixing dinner. Time after time, Dad would come home and greet Mom in the kitchen. Their conversation would go on for some time about their respective days. Almost without fail, Mom would say something positive to Dad about something I had done that day such as:

"You won't believe what Steve has built this time. It is great!"

"You've got to see the good marks Steve got on his assignment today. He is such a good student."

"Steve is the most focused child I have ever seen. He always sticks to whatever he is doing until it is finished."

I'm sure Mom knew exactly what she was doing. I'm sure at some point along the way that I did too! But the expectation was clear and the reinforcement was powerful.

Mom understood this powerful principle of molding positive behavior:

Praise in public. Let the whole world overhear--especially your young person!

But remember to discipline in private. Never air your frustrations about your children where others can overhear-- especially your children. What you say positively or negatively about them where they can overhear creates the expectation for their future behavior.

Dealing with negative behavior in a positive way. As a simple example of a powerful principle, let's take a look at the case of the messy room. Every parent has had to deal with children who won't pick up after themselves. How the problem is dealt with is an indication of how this and other behavior problems can and should be handled.

Instead of saying: "Your room is always so messy." (Negative expectation)

Start saying: "This doesn't look like the room of someone as responsible as you are." (Positive expectation)

Instead of saying: "You are so disorganized." (Negative character expectation)

Start saying: "You know how important being clean and organized is. I know you can do it." (Positive character and behavior expectation)

It has been said in the past, criticize the behavior, not the person. That is a good start. But...

If you want to create positive expectations for both behavior and the person, then communicate your high expectations for both.

What's in a Name?

Names and labels are two powerful character and behavior shaping tools. Give children a bad name and they will live up to it. Give them a good name and they will most likely live up to that as well.

The character game: All the youngsters at our house wait with great anticipation for bedtime. The routine is similar each night with each child--story time, prayers, a game, and then a song. A game? Let me explain because it gets high marks from the kids.

Each night after they are tucked into bed we play a different game. Each game involves lots of communication and mind activity--not much physical activity since we're working to get everyone settled down for the night!

One of the favorites is the Character Game. We go through each letter of the alphabet and take turns naming a character trait that starts with that letter. It goes something like this:

> Dad: "Abby is **a**mbitious."
> Abby: "Abby is **b**eautiful!"
> Dad: "Abby is **c**aring."
> Abby: "Abby is....What is a word that starts with **d**?"
> Dad: "Determined."
> Abby: "What is determined?"
> Dad: "You stick with the task until you get it done and never give up."

And so it goes through the whole alphabet. It becomes a vocabulary builder as well as a character builder. She has twenty-six positive character traits to think about all night long! It gives her high expectations and a great name to live up to.

Variation on a theme for older kids: Every once in a while we do an activity in our company where we gather everyone together in the conference room. One person acts as scribe at the easel pad. We write a person's name at the top of the large piece of easel pad paper and then the others present take turns calling out a positive word that describes that person. The scribe writes all of the words on the paper. When it is full we tear the sheet off and give it to that person.

Those sheets usually end up hanging somewhere prominent in that person's work area for all to see. They stay there for months!

For teenagers, try something similar. It might even take place around the dinner table where everyone takes a turn naming a positive character trait about a specific member of the family. It may sound corny at first, but just watch the magic unfold as the expectations are stated and character is built.

Remember--**Give them a great name to live up to.**

Planting a Seed for Positive Future Behavior

Remember my mom the gardener? Besides being a great seed planter in the garden as well as in the mind with positive overhear psychology, she was a master at planting positive expectations for future behavior.

Nearing my sixteenth birthday, Mom and I were in the car going somewhere together. She was driving. She asked if I was looking forward to getting my driver's license. The conversation continued. Somewhere along the way she made a point that sunk deep into my heart and mind when she said, **"I know you are going to be the best driver in the family."**

Now that was a tall order to fill considering I am the last of seven children. But it created a very high expectation for me to live up to. Her expression of confidence in me painted a very vivid vision of what she expected my future behavior to be.

Unfortunately, the more common approach would be for a parent to express anxiety over the prospect of licensing, worry about the new driver being adequately practiced, and worry over exposure to potential accidents. Doubt and concern only project a lack of confidence and low expectations. That gives great license to really mess up. After all, that is what is expected!

To get more of the behavior you want, express your confidence in your young people's ability to perform and rise to the occasion--and they usually will!

Gratitude--The Ultimate Expectation Builder

One of my favorite things we do in our seminars is to give everyone an "I appreciate" pad. The assignment is for each person to write as many sincere thank you notes or expressions of appreciation to as many people as possible during the course. It is amazing to see the behavior change when these notes start going to the service help in the hotel. A little recognition goes a long way toward ensuring great service!

Every once in a while, different members of our family will find an "I appreciate" note written to them from their dad. These are left sitting somewhere conspicuous where they will be found easily. Gratitude for the little things--especially in recognition of character traits--goes a long way toward reinforcing great behavior and giving any person--young or old-- high expectations to live up to.

Remember: **Recognize and express appreciation for the positive behavior and character traits you want and you'll usually get more of them!**

Are You Setting High Expectations?

How are you setting up a high expectation environment in your home?

- ☐ Do you use positive overhear psychology to plant the seeds of positive expectations?

- ☐ Do you deal with negative behavior in a positive way?

- ☐ Do you give your young person a great name to live up to?

- ☐ Do you plant seeds for positive future behavior?

- ☐ Do you express gratitude and appreciation for the positive behavior and character traits you see?

Remember: In life, you usually get what you expect!

MISTAKE 4
Having a House with No "Walls"

We recently took a short family history trip to upstate New York. We visited several historical towns and sites, one of which was an old farm house built in the early 1800's. It was very small and built out of logs with two stories and almost no internal structures or walls. We were told that a family of thirteen lived in that house at one time nearly 200 years ago.

I could only imagine what that must have been like--all those people under one roof with little or no space to themselves. The cramped quarters must have created some tense situations, especially in the dead of winter when there was nowhere else to go but in the house. The "walls" of discipline and self-control must have been tremendous for everyone to coexist happily in that house with no internal physical walls.

Our homes today by comparison are opulent mansions. A two bedroom house with a kitchen and living room is many times the house that the cabin in New York was. Yet as we have gained more space and more internal physical walls, the "walls" or limits of discipline have come tumbling down.

The case of Rebecca: It all started when Rebecca was very young. Bedtime was a battle. She never wanted to go to bed and held out as long as she possibly could! The bedtime battle lasted at least two hours every night. She would continue to get up, ask for a drink of water, complain she couldn't sleep, and demand another story or she would not go to bed!

Similar behavior developed as she got older. Many times when asked to do something, she would roll her eyes or even refuse to do it--so she didn't have to. She found tattling to be an effective tool to deflect the attention away from herself so she could get what she wanted while getting others in trouble.

When she got a little older, she refused to wear the clothes her mother bought for her. They had to be the clothes of her choice if she was going to wear them. Her parents complied and did it her way even though her tastes were much more expensive and radical.

And so her life continued with her parents always giving her whatever she wanted. Since there were very few "walls" or boundaries at home, as she got older and ventured out into the world, she behaved as though the world revolved around her. She would spend years learning a lesson she should have learned early on--there are walls or boundaries in life.

Little Kenneth and "his" food: Little Kenneth had quite a life. Each night, from a very early age, his mother would fix him a special dinner with just the things he liked while the rest of the family ate the regular dinner she had prepared. Because he would not eat vegetables as a little boy, his mother was afraid he was not eating enough, so she catered to his tastes in order to get enough food into him.

This routine continued until Kenneth left for college. Mom was still cooking just for him because he would not eat like everyone else. Since Kenneth could not take his mom to college to fix his special meals, he took to fast food most of his college days because that's what he liked. It may take years for him to understand that the rest of world is not going to be so willing to cater to his every whim-- especially his future employer and his future wife!

Left unchecked with no "walls" or boundaries, we all tend to keep pushing in order to get whatever we think we want.

There is something that we were born with that gives us the desire to know where our boundaries are. If you have ever worked with animals, you have seen it in action. When you put a cow in a new pasture, she will walk slowly around the fence line and push at the wire and the poles to see if there are any outlets. She then knows that she has access only to the grass that is within the boundaries of the fence.

We all have that same inclination. That may help to explain why Columbus headed out over the ocean, not being sure what was out there. It is likely why Lewis and Clark explored the Great West, the Wright Brothers tried to fly, and Chuck Yeager broke the sound barrier. They all wanted to know where the boundaries were and how far they could go before they ran into limits they could not get past.

Even though the boundaries of our earth were determined, at least geographically, we sent Neal Armstrong into outer space to see what was out there. And we're still pushing out--now beyond our solar system.

Human nature wants to know where the limits are. Too often, however, parents who are charged with setting up boundaries never do it. So just like the great explorers, children keep testing, pushing and exploring and at least subconsciously wondering where the limits are. Not having any boundaries at home, they strike out on their own to see where the limits are in the schoolroom, in extracurricular activities, at work and in the community. They just keep pushing until someone or something resists and they learn a lesson the hard way that could have been avoided if boundaries had been set for them earlier at home.

Learning where the boundaries are--the hard way. Several years ago, two teenage boys who lived in the small south central Texas town we lived in at the time, put two sealed plastic gallon milk jugs filled with dry ice on the roof of the local high school during a Friday night dance. Then they took off. When the pressure exceeded the strength of the plastic jugs, they exploded making a very loud bomb-like sound. There was no damage, but it did create some commotion and frightened a few of the girls at the dance. At the time it was taken by most as a rather inventive practical joke.

Just four days later, however, the shooting disaster at Columbine High School in Colorado occurred and heightened everyone's sensitivity to school security. Taking a cue from this changed public attitude, the local sheriff set out to assure the citizens that nothing like that would ever happen in our community. They chose to do it by making an example of the two practical jokers from the weekend before.

Because the boys had bragged about their prank to too many people, they were easily identified, arrested and jailed. For our small town of 30,000 this was big news, and it made the front page of the local paper for several days.

Then came the parental reaction. "The system was not fair; it was totally corrupt; the authorities were over-reacting; it was just a practical joke." This was also the verbal defense of the two students.

The law, however, looked at everything very differently. This was an act of vandalism on government property--a felony offense. As the investigation progressed, it was discovered that these two students had been on numerous web sites where they had learned how to make bombs. One of the boys had frequently worn army fatigues to school and seemed, from outside appearances, to be overly interested in guns and explosives. To investigators, it appeared as if there were few boundaries at home and a lack of parental supervision.

The sheriff justified her actions by saying that her department prevented what could have been a major catastrophe. She said this was just a sign of worse things to come from these boys unless someone taught them where the boundaries were.

As a result, these boys learned about boundaries the hard way with a year and a half of probation and time in the local alternative school with other kids who had been expelled from the public school system.

Both would have been much better off learning valuable lessons about boundaries at home instead of at the hands of the law.

If you don't create boundaries, someone else will. The principal of our local high school in a Dallas, Texas, suburb has some very strict rules for the school's athletes. For example, if an athlete is found at any type of function where alcohol is being served, he is expelled from the team. The principal's reasoning, however, is not what you would expect. He says that since most parents don't set high enough standards and clear boundaries with their teenage children, he feels the need to do it for them.

The house with no "walls" has little discipline or boundaries for behavior. What never gets taught at home will probably have to be learned the hard way--by trial and error in the bigger world where learning those lessons is far more expensive and painful.

SOLUTION
Create a Happy Home with Strong "Walls"

Another history lesson: Whenever we are in San Antonio, Texas, our family loves to visit the Alamo--the cradle of Texas liberty. On one of our first visits, our oldest daughter had just completed several weeks of lessons on Texas history. As we approached, she said, "Where's the line?" When I inquired about what she was referring to, she didn't have the time or patience to explain, she just set off to find it. She said, "I know it's around here somewhere."

When she found it, she got very excited, especially because the line had been preserved in metal and imbedded in stone in front of the Alamo. A plaque nearby explained the significance of the line. It turns out that those in the fort (the Alamo) were waiting anxiously for reinforcements from Texas General Sam Houston. When the fort was obviously going to be under siege from General Santa Anna of Mexico, Colonel William Barnett Travis took his sword and drew a line in the dirt between himself and his troops. He then announced that everyone who was willing to follow him and fight for Texas independence was to step over the line and join him. He said if any didn't want to step over the line and follow him, they could leave and find safety elsewhere. Colonel Travis was a great leader and great leaders expect high standards from their troops. They know how to set the boundaries for the behavior they want.

What fascinated me most about the experience we had as a family was our daughter's fascination with that famous line and her desire to find it. She was not satisfied or happy with our visit until she saw where the "boundary" was.

One of my first clear memories about boundaries happened when I was very young. Mom had just asked me to do something. Either in an unthinking moment, or in a typical exploration of where the boundaries were, I told her "No." Dad, however, was within earshot at the time. I will never forget that my dad, who is traditionally soft spoken, came seemingly from out of nowhere, looked straight at me and said, "You don't say 'No' to your mother." I discovered a boundary that day. It was a boundary I never crossed again. It was the last time I ever said "No" to my mother!

It was very clear to me that day what my father's position was on my behavior toward my mother. Since it was clear in his own mind, his communication with me was just as clear. Just like Colonel Travis at the Alamo, there was no mistake about where he stood.

How clear are you about the behavior expectations in your home? Exactly where do you stand on the following behaviors?

- ❑ Talking back.

- ❑ Tattling.

- ❑ Gossiping.

- ❑ Saying "No" when asked to do something.

- ❑ Not responding immediately when asked to do something.

- ❑ Rolling eyes when being counseled or asked to do something.

❏ Putting off chores or responsibilities and having to be asked repeatedly.

❏ Not coming home on time.

❏ Not letting you know where they are and when they will be home.

❏ Not being grateful for the things they are given.

❏ Exhibiting an attitude of "it's never good enough" when things are given to them or done for them--for things as simple as a meal that is cooked for them or a gift that is given to them.

❏ Frequently complaining "It's not fair."

❏ Being unkind in communication or treatment of other family members.

The problem of the house with no "walls" begins with the lack of decision on the part of parents about the specific things that are and are not acceptable. If you are not clear, how do you ever expect your children to be?

"Up with which you will not put!" That's a phrase coined by Winston Churchill somewhere back in history when someone criticized his grammar. It seems very appropriate here. Several years ago when our company was still in its infancy, we all sat down and did an exercise that laid the foundation for the culture in our organization. All team members were given a piece of paper and asked to write down a list of all the behaviors they would not put up with from others in the office. We then discussed each person's list. It was the initial step we took to understand where each other's boundaries were. While it took several years to create the culture we wanted, starting with those personal boundaries was a very productive first step.

A similar exercise might be well advised at home.

Step #1 to Building a House with Strong "Walls"
Set Clear Boundaries

With your spouse, ask yourselves:

> **1.** What are the behavioral boundaries in our home?

> **2.** What behaviors do we expect from our children?

> **3.** What behaviors "up with which we will not put?"

Clarity in your own minds is the first step toward creating a family culture with clear boundaries and expectations.

Communicating the rules of the game: We love to play board games at our house. The whole family gets together at least once a week and we play a different game. Sometimes it takes only half an hour, but everyone participates.

Whenever we play a new game, everyone wants to know what the rules are. Once I made the mistake of telling everyone that I would explain the rules as we went along instead of taking the time to explain everything up front.

It was disaster!

I spent most of the time telling everyone that they could not do this or could not do that. With no clear rules or boundaries set from the beginning, I became the bad guy having to watch each person's every move. It was frustrating and no fun for anyone.

The next time we played a game together, we took the time to go over the rules so everyone understood them before we started. Knowing exactly where the boundaries were ahead of time, we were all so much happier because we knew how to play the game successfully. It was fun, exciting, and a great family experience.

What applies to the board game applies to the home in general. I'm always amazed at how much happier children of all ages (as well as adults, for that matter) seem to be when they clearly understand what the expectations and boundaries are at home, at school, and at work.

Step #2 to Building a House with Strong "Walls"
Communicate Clearly What the Boundaries Are

Once you are clear in your own mind what the boundaries are, communicating them to everyone else is the next task.

In your children's early years, clarity in your own mind is 80% of the battle. When you are clear, you will arrest improper behavior as soon as it emerges by clear communication and proper consequences. Here are some examples:

Rebecca and bedtime: Instead of engaging in the bedtime battle, Rebecca is given a clear boundary:

> "Rebecca, it is time to go to bed. We are going
> to read a story, say our prayers and sing a song
> together. Then it will be time for you to go to sleep.
> If you are not ready to sleep, you may sit or lie
> quietly in your bed and look at a book, but you
> are not to get out of bed or come out of your
> room."

The first attempts to get out of bed are met with a consistent response of taking her back and reinforcing the boundary. After a few nights of consistency, she'll get the message.

The problem comes in those first few nights when parents are tempted to cave into crying, whining and other attempts to test the boundaries.

Kenneth and his eating habits: Kenneth does not want to eat his dinner and wants something else instead. The clear communication of the boundary might go something like this:

> "Kenneth, this is what we are having for dinner
> tonight. You may eat what has been prepared
> or you may choose not to. It's your choice, but

this is what we are having. As soon as dinner is
over, there will be no snacks or meal until
breakfast tomorrow. The decision is yours."

Kenneth now has a decision to make. He may hold out tonight and
maybe tomorrow night, but eventually he will learn that if he is
hungry, he better eat what has been prepared–now! It is amazing
how fast kids learn to love vegetables and healthy food when the
system is set up correctly!

Clearly communicate the boundaries for behavior including choices
and consequences.

Step #3 in Building a House with Strong "Walls"
Include Your Children in the Creation of the Rules in Your Home and the Consequences for Crossing Set Boundaries

As children get older and progress into young adulthood, another
natural law comes into play that can be employed as boundaries are
defined and reinforced. It says:

**People believe the solutions they have created or discovered
themselves more than the solutions given to them by others.**

With your guidance, allow everyone in the family to participate in
creating the "rules of the game" in your home. The more ownership
they have in the design, the more enthusiasm they will have for
compliance.

As soon as children are old enough to communicate and understand
-- at about age five or six--you can have a discussion about what is
appropriate behavior. This discussion can be repeated as children
get older and new experiences come into the picture. The discussion
about their responsibility for their own rooms might go like this:

How should you keep your room?

Why is it important to keep it neat and clean?

How do you feel when it is neat and clean?

In case you forget to keep it neat and clean, what do you think would be an appropriate consequence?

The consequence question may require some help on your part, but in general, most children are clear on what is the right thing to do.

The earlier you start these discussions, the easier they become as the years pass. You can use the same system at every stage of development. For example:

Why do you think it is important that we all communicate where we are going and when we will be home?

Why do you think we believe it is important to be home before midnight?

In the unlikely event that you might choose not to be home by midnight, what do you think the appropriate consequence should be?

Again, you may have to prompt some of the answers to each question and create some of the rules and consequences, but the dynamic is the same. Make your children part of the discussion and part of the solution. The more they feel ownership in it, the more they will be willing to live with it and comply.

Step #4 in Building a House with Strong "Walls"
Follow Through, Be Consistent, and Let the Previously Agreed upon Rules Be the Taskmaster--not You

Once the "rules of the game" are established along with the consequences and they are made clear to everyone, the rest is just playing by those rules. If boundaries are crossed or rules violated, the previously agreed upon consequences become the taskmaster --not you. But consistency is important.

Example: You have agreed with your teenage son that curfew is midnight. The agreed upon consequence for stepping over that boundary is loss of car privileges for a week.

Friday night he comes in at 12:15 a.m. Your only comment is this: "Son, I'm glad you are home safe and sound. We were worried about you. You know what we agreed about curfew so I am sure you will make your plans without the car for the next week. I know you'll do better next time."

The important thing is consistency in following the rules. No matter the excuse, the rules and consequences stand firm. That is what you all agreed to. Just as in the board game, if the rules are clearly communicated up front, then those involved know how to play the game and they know the consequences for not following the rules. Reinforce strong "walls" by letting the previously agreed upon rules be the taskmaster–not you! When boundaries are crossed, you are just following the rules as you expect your children to do.

The Benefit of Building a House with Strong "Walls"

Early understanding and continual reinforcement of rules and consequences builds a strong foundation for life. In every area of life there are rules and consequences:

- at home
- at school
- at work
- in the community
- in the country

The earlier everyone understands this principle, the faster and better he or she will progress in every area of life. So in order to create a firm foundation for life for your children, start by building strong "walls" or boundaries at home by doing the following:

1. Get clear in your own mind what the boundaries and expectations are in your home.

2. Clearly communicate the boundaries for behavior including choices and consequences.

3. Include your age appropriate young people in the creation

of the rules of the game and the consequences for crossing the boundaries; let them have ownership in the rules and the consequences.

4. Reinforce strong "walls" by letting the previously agreed upon rules and consequences be the taskmaster–not you! When boundaries are crossed, follow the rules as you expect your children to do! Be consistent!

MISTAKE 5
Being a Victim of Approval Addiction and Passing It on to Your Children

Except for the fear of death, the fear of rejection is one of the greatest fears we have.

No one wants to be:
> * rejected,
> * scorned,
> * criticized,
> * ignored,
> * discounted or
> * taken for granted.

Everyone wants to be:
> * admired,
> * praised,
> * recognized,
> * important and
> * appreciated.

It is natural to seek the things we want and to avoid the things we don't want. However, when acceptance and the approval of others become an overpowering motivation, people do all kinds of things that they would not otherwise rationally do, or they fail to do things they should do unless they can see a way that they will receive some kind of praise and recognition. This malady begins with parents and carries over into the lives of their children. We are going to talk about **three kinds of approval addiction:**

(1) parents' need for the approval of their friends and neighbors;

(2) parents' need for the approval of their children;

(3) children becoming dependent on parental approval for motivation.

Approval Addiction 1
Parents' Need for the Approval of Other People

Do you feel the approval of others is necessary? Do you feel it is important to look good in the sight of:
* friends,
* neighbors,
* family members,
* the parents of your children's friends,
* your children's school teachers,
* your own children?

Measure your own level of approval addiction by checking any of the following statements you have thought or heard yourself say to the young people in your life:

* "You're not going to embarrass the family that way."

* "You look ridiculous in that. Everyone will think you have a mother who doesn't know how to dress you. Go and change."

* "You can't go out with him/her. What will people think?"

* "I hope no one else saw these grades."

* "Will you please get the lawn mowed. The neighbors will think we are a bunch of slobs."

* "That hair is ridiculous. You are not going to be seen at the dance like that in front of the whole town."

* "How could you have said that? Everyone is going to think you have parents who don't teach their children good manners."

What is the message here? With consistent reinforcement, the message is this: **"What really matters most is what other people think."**

Since the natural tendency is for all teenagers to be peer motivated, just add an extra dose of your own approval addiction and they will get a double dose of the message that what other people think matters most. Compound that over the years and you will have adults who are so focused on the opinions of others that they'll have a very difficult time ever deciding what it is best for themselves.

Consider these facts:

* The number one factor that influences most graduating high school students in their choice of a college is where their friends are going or what their friends are doing.

* One of the main reasons college students choose the college major they do is because it sounds impressive to other people or it is what their parents want or expect.

* A major factor in the career choice college students make is that it sounds prestigious to other people.

Being approval addicted and being overly focused on what other people think is one of the single greatest contributing factors to poor career choices and unhappiness in life.

Approval Addiction 2
Parents' Need for the Approval of Their Own Children

Approval addiction takes on another dimension when parents allow their direction or judgment to be altered because an idea or course of action won't meet with their children's approval.

Do you exhibit any of the symptoms of being addicted to the approval of your children? Check off any of the following that might apply to you:

* I want to know what my children say about me
to their friends and their friends' parents.

* It bothers me when my children are upset or mad
at me so I cave in to doing whatever I need to
do to please them.

* I want my children to be good, but I don't want
them to think I am too strict.

* I tend to give my children material things to make
up for lack of time and attention I give them.

* I like to be "one of the guys" or "one of the gals"
with my preteen or teenage children and their
friends.

* I don't push my children as much as I could
because I don't want them to resent me.

* I probably let them get away with more than I
should.

* I want my children's friends to think that I am
"cool."

* I don't ask my children too many questions
because I don't want them to think I'm prying
or being nosey.

* I let my children have their own space and I
don't bother them too much.

* I don't even ask my children to do things around
the house anymore because it is too much of a
hassle to get them to do it. It's easier just to do it
myself.

* I don't want my children to have to go through

what I did when I was their age. I just want them to have fun while they can.

While there is probably nothing wrong with any one of these things by itself, the combined effect of more than one can be a signal that you are addicted to the approval of your children.

If one of your first objectives is to be your child's "buddy," loss of respect from your children is close at hand.

Listen to what some teenage Eagle "U" students have to say about parents who are addicted to their children's approval:

☐ "My mom is such a pushover. I can get anything I want from her if I just get a little upset. She doesn't want me to be mad at her."

☐ "I think my dad must feel guilty that he spends so much time at work. All I have to do if I want money, the car or anything else is just ask him for some of his time. He'd rather give me something to keep me happy."

☐ "The magic phrase for me is 'Michele's parents are letting her go' and everything else falls into place. My parents don't ever want me to be able to say that they were the cause of my being left out."

☐ "My parents let me do just about anything I want. I can get away with anything."

☐ "All my friends say my parents are pretty 'cool' because they let me stay out late, take the car whenever I want it, and do whatever I want to do."

Ironically these are the same young people who have little or no respect for their parents. And when respect is gone, positive influence goes right along with it.

Approval Addiction 3
Having Your Children Addicted to Your Approval

Having children who want to please their parents can be a real blessing, especially if it translates into their doing what is morally right. But when young people become addicted to their parents' approval in other areas such as:

* extracurricular activities,
* athletics,
* courses of study in school,
* the college they choose,
* the college major they select,
* or the career they pursue,

it can create all kinds of unhappiness and misdirection now and in their future.

Wrestling with his dad's expectations: Ben's dad was a great high school and college wrestler. He would often tell of his victories and how much he looked forward to seeing his son do the same things he did.   When Ben finally got to high school it was just assumed that he would go out for wrestling, which he did.   But it became obvious to the other team members that Ben was there for his dad, not for himself.   He had very little enthusiasm during practice and frequently got injured or sick. He was miserable most of the time, but kept on doing it for four years because he knew it would devastate his dad if he didn't.

Sara and the sorority trap: Sara's mother was a very prominent figure in the community and very well known among the most influential women in town.   She had been the president of "the" sorority many years before at the local university.   Since Sara was a legacy (daughter of a sorority alumna), everyone, and especially her mother, expected her to join that sorority.   When she was actively rushed by another group--the one most of her friends were going to join--Sara's mother let it be known that Sara was going to join her sorority. Thus, when the other options had been eliminated and not wanting to disappoint her mother, Sara went along with her desires.

He's just not a "chip off the old block": A very successful surgeon urged his son to pursue a career in medicine and join him in his practice. The son was an excellent student and made it through medical school with flying colors. When he got into the practical side of performing surgery, however, his performance was substandard. He seemed to be all thumbs. His doctor/father came down on him very hard, saying that he must not be trying hard enough and that he could do it if he just applied himself.

It was ultimately discovered that the son did not have his father's finger dexterity nor did the son enjoy working with patients who were under sedation. He was pursuing the specialty because it pleased his father, but in reality he had very little interest or natural ability in that area.

Do what his dad wants him to do or else: Rick's father came from a very poor family. He was one of the first in his family to graduate from college and then graduate school. He became a successful family practice physician. Because of his personal experience, he expected all of his children to get a graduate level education and go into one of the professions. He paid their way through college. He even bought them each a car and a condo for their college years. They had no excuse not to get an education and become some type of a professional.

Rick, however, discovered in college that the thing he enjoyed most was coaching basketball. But since his dad had invested so much money in his education and threatened to take away the car and the condo if he did not follow through on getting a law degree, Rick did not dare go against his father's wishes. He got his law degree, and continues to bounce around from firm to firm and job to job being very unhappy and unfulfilled in his career.

What Messages Are You Secretly Sending?

How often do you assume and/or communicate subtly, or not so subtly, the following to your young people? "I know you'll--

* follow in my foot steps,

* make me proud,

* take over the family business some day,

* do better in my profession than I did,

* carry on the family tradition or

* be a professional like I am."

These messages and others like them may be setting your own children up to be approval addicted and ultimately very unhappy and unfulfilled by being trapped in something that Mom or Dad wanted but something in which they have little or no interest.

Is Approval Addiction Attacking You or Your Young People In Any of These Three Areas?

1. **Becoming addicted to the approval of others.**
   How concerned are you really about what the Joneses think? Is there anything in your communication or in your behavior with your young people that would lead them to believe that what matters most is what everyone else thinks?

   If you are trying to motivate with messages of looking good to others for your sake, you are communicating that you are motivated by what others think. You can expect that your children will follow your example and eventually be more and more motivated by what their own peers think of them.

2. **Becoming addicted to the approval of your children.**
   To what degree do you seek the approval of your children? Do you ever let them off easy so they won't dislike you or give you a hassle? Are you trying too hard to be their buddy?

   If you try to motivate by permissiveness and letting them do as they please, the lack of direction from you may translate into a lack of direction for them.

3. **Causing your children to be addicted to your approval.**
   Are your children addicted to your approval? Are they making their educational, extracurricular, and/or career choices for **you** or because it is the right fit for **them** and their talents and abilities?

If you try to motivate your children by getting them to please you and by telling them what to do, you may cripple them for a lifetime. They may go along with your desires today and be miserable all their lives, and/or they may show little or no motivation to do anything significant unless there is someone to praise and reinforce them.

Some approval tactics may motivate some of the time for some of the people, but they carry high risks for the future emotional health and success of young people.

SOLUTION
Transform Approval Addiction into Self-motivation

Every parent wants children who are self-motivated, successful and self-reliant. Nearly every day at Eagle "U" we receive calls from parents who ask, "How can I motivate my young people to take more responsibility for their own future success?"

First of all, it is important to understand that you cannot motivate your young people to do anything.

You may demand, threaten, manipulate, cajole, or coerce and get an immediate result, but at what expense? It will probably be at the expense of their future happiness and success.

There is a natural law that remains consistent in human behavior no matter the age of the individual. It is that **people are motivated by their own reasoning--not by that of anyone else.**

You can only find out what it is that motivates your children, and then create the environment in which their self-motivation is stimulated.

Instead of perpetuating approval addiction on each of the three fronts discussed earlier, let's see how we can transform approval addiction into self-motivation.

Helping Young People to Work on Their Own Self-image

The more concerned we are with what others think about us, the more we look outside ourselves to others for a feeling of acceptance and approval. Those who are secure in their own self-image and self-worth are seldom influenced by the random opinions of others. They rarely allow other people to cause them to feel unapproved of.

Plant firmly in the minds of your young people a clear image of their potential and of who they really are.

Here's how:

Motivation for good grades: We all want our children to get good grades. But are children concerned with them? Maybe they aren't if they see no relevance between grades and what they want.

Example: A boy whom we shall call Michael only has interest as a high school student in his band. He wants to be a rock star. So why should he waste his time with non-music subjects or worry about his grades? That's what he wants to know. You know that good grades will keep his options open in the future. So how do you motivate him without making all of the approval addiction mistakes?

1. Reinforce a positive self-image and the belief that he can accomplish anything he wants to if he puts his mind to it, makes a plan, and follows through.

2. Ask him what he thinks it is going to take to be successful in music (or anything else for that matter) and what he needs to do right now to prepare for that career.   In addition to needing to acquire knowledge of music, how it is written, what makes a good song, he'll need a knowledge of computers and technology in order to edit and produce a good product. He'll need a knowledge of people and what they like and don't like so he'll know how to promote himself. Help him make a list of as many things as the two of you can come up with.

Remember, you are helping him to create a plan for success. He needs to see you as a supporter, not a critic, even if you don't agree with the exact direction he might be taking at the moment   The lessons learned in the process could be invaluable.

3. Reinforce that the best route is going to be for him to get all of the best knowledge available to him today through school and any other means he can so he will be successful in every aspect of music tomorrow, assuming that is what he ultimately chooses.

4. Next, set up the system and the rules of the game. Advise him to put in the right amount of preparation so he will then have time to do more of what he wants to do. Point out that if he will study and make the grades, it will be smooth sailing for his music. If the grades drop, then the band takes a backseat until the grades come back up. Those are the conditions and the rules for success.

5. Continually reinforce your belief in him--that he is a good student, that he can have anything in life he wants if he follows the steps to get there.

If Michael's study time starts slipping along with some of his test scores, the best response might be, "I'm surprised. These grades don't look like your grades. You are a great student. I know how much you enjoy your music. How can I help you follow through on what you need to do?"

Imagine the self-image of the young person who hears comments like these on a regular basis:

"I know you can do it."

"You can accomplish whatever you want when you follow the system for getting it."

"It's your decision. All you have to do is go after it."

Instead of communicating approval addiction, do the following:

1. Find out what really motivates your young people.

2. Help them discover the path to get there.

3. Set up the system so the right steps are in place for them to learn life-time lessons for success.

4. Reinforce a positive self-image and self-worth regularly.

Parents who are addicted to their children's approval have the misconception that love is permissiveness or that the more they give, the more their children will love, respect and obey them.

The opposite is true. Love is not permissiveness. Your children don't need a buddy. They need a parent!

When I was in high school, I pushed pretty hard for the school to implement some type of teacher evaluation where the students could give teachers anonymous feedback as well as cast their vote for the best teachers in the school. The administration was reluctant for fear the students would just vote for the teachers they liked the most because they were easiest on them instead of the ones who were really doing a great teaching job.

After a lot of discussion with the administration, they agreed to testing the idea. Each student was given a ballot and the votes were cast for the best teacher in the school.

It came as no surprise to us that one of the first winners was Julie

Hewlett. Ms. Hewlett had been my piano teacher when I was in the eighth grade. When I got to high school, she was the teacher of the freshman and sophomore choirs as well as the teacher of a course in humanities. She was known for her high performance standards, her "tough love," and her unwillingness to accept anything but the best from her students. Virtually every honor roll student clamored to get into her humanities class. It was always filled to capacity with a waiting list. All of the stars on the football team were in her music class. She demanded as much or more from them in their efforts in her class as the football coaches did from them on the football field.

Many days we would leave her class shaking our heads or complaining about her unrealistically high standards for excellence and her burdensome homework loads. The process was not always enjoyable. But the end result was a sense of accomplishment and achievement that made it all worth it. We all knew that she demanded so much of us because she believed in us more than we believed in ourselves sometimes. And for that we revered her and respected her as one of the best educators in the school and in our lives.

We love and respect most those who believe in us and expect the most from us, not those who let us off easy and just let us get by.

Be a parental source of guidance and motivation when your children are young and you'll have great friends when they reach adulthood. Be your children's buddy when they are young and you will be raising those children for the rest of your life!

Focus on their future success instead of their approval by:

* Setting high standards for them to live up to.

* Continually reinforcing your belief that they can accomplish the things they set out to do. Keep saying, "I know you can do it."

* Setting up the system for them to succeed. Help them develop a plan to accomplish their goals--what **they** want. Then be their biggest cheerleader and coach to help them get there. Let the

system be the disciplinarian. Don't make the rules up as you go along.

* Expressing your belief in them on those occasions when they quit believing in themselves.

* Holding them to a higher standard than those around them. "You can do better than the average."

* Loving them when they seem quite unlovable. When they are discouraged, angry, want to quit, slip up, and blame you, pour it on! Hold the line and keep reinforcing your belief in them.

* Giving them your time and attention instead of giving them things. Focus on helping them to be their best. The greatest gift you can give is your belief in them.

* Giving them plenty to do around the house. Let them know they are valuable members of the family and that their contribution is vital.

Be sure your young people achieve to please themselves, not just to please you.

John came to Eagle "U" as a college student. He was raised in a very strict home where his parents imposed high standards. They demanded the best and allowed him little freedom to do anything but what they expected. His parents set the standards and rules and were the disciplinarians. They were very proud of his good behavior and accomplishments in high school.

By the time John was suddenly on his own in college, he had been working for his parents for so long and had been pushed so hard, he just laid back and enjoyed his new-found freedom. He was in rebellion without even realizing it. He stayed out late, started drinking, and fell in with other unmotivated students. His parents could not understand it. It was almost like he had become a different person.

Michael was in the same class with John at Eagle "U." He too had parents who had high standards and expectations. Michael's parents, however, had worked with him to set his goals. They discussed with him what he wanted to accomplish. They gave him suggestions and planted in his mind their belief in his potential.

Together they came up with a plan to reach his goals and the steps to get there. Together they set up a system so that he could succeed. Michael had great freedom to make his own decisions, knowing full well exactly what the consequences of each of those decisions would be before he ever made them. He and the system were the disciplinarians. His parents just reinforced the agreements they had made together.

Michael's performance in high school, like John's, was outstanding. But unlike John, when Michael got to college, he excelled in every area. He used everything he had learned at home to get ahead in college. He was working for his own satisfaction and sense of accomplishment, not that of his parents. The preparation that Michael's parents gave him propelled him to even greater accomplishment after he left home.

How you set up the system and the messages you send have everything to do with your young people's success in the present and in the future. Are they doing it for you and learning to be addicted to your approval, or are they doing it because you have given them an understanding of the value of self-satisfaction and a sense of accomplishment?

What messages are you sending about whom your children are pleasing? Here are some examples of transforming your language from pleasing you to getting self-satisfaction from a job well done:

Change "You make me so proud" **to** "It must feel great to have accomplished your goal."

Change "Be a professional like I am" **to** "You can be the best at whatever you choose to do."

Change "Take over the family business some day" **to** "You have a lot of options. Let's weigh them carefully and find the thing that fits you best."

Change "Follow in my footsteps" **to** "You can set a high standard in whatever you decide to do."

Change "Do better in my profession than I have" **to** "You will do the best at whatever you choose to do."

There is great value in carrying on the family tradition of being honest, hard working, having integrity, taking initiative, etc. Parents often do better at teaching these values than at helping their children select the appropriate career path.

You are responsible for the elimination of approval addiction in all its forms. This is accomplished when you understand that you are responsible to help your young people become self-reliant, responsible and successful in the way that fits their natural abilities and talents the best. It all starts with the understanding that they aren't you in talent, interest or ability.

Here are some things to remember:

* They can't embarrass you in front of the neighbors because they aren't you.

* You can't love them by being permissive and giving them whatever they want, and they certainly won't love you for it if you do.

* They can't please you by pursuing your interests in your life because they aren't you.

Inside of them rests a unique ability to do something extraordinary in their own way. Help them find it. Encourage them to be the best at whatever they decide to do at whatever age they might be. Help them create high standards for themselves and follow through to help them live up to those standards.

The best approval they could ever have is the satisfaction of seeing a job well done, of setting high standards and living up to them, of being the best at whatever they set out to do.

Self-satisfaction--knowing that they are fulfilling their greatest potential--is the most satisfying form of approval that you can give the young people in your life.

Eliminate Approval Addiction

1. Find out what motivates your children. What do they really want? Get to know them and their wants, desires and ambitions.

2. Plant firmly in the minds of your young people a clear image of their potential--of who they really are.

3. Help them discover the path to get there.

4. Set up the system so the right steps are in place for them to learn life-time lessons of success.

5. Reinforce a positive self-image and self-worth regularly.

6. Remember that love is not permissiveness. Set high standards with them and hold them to it. They will love you for it later!

7. Create in them a desire for self-reliance and self-satisfaction by working to uncover their unique ability. They aren't you! You aren't they. They are themselves!

MISTAKE 6
Accepting Average

Being healthy on average. The first time I had my blood work reviewed by Jack Fairchild who is a Certified Clinical Nutritionist, he proceeded to cross out all of the numbers in the average or normal range column of the report. The theory for having this column is that it provides a range within which one should fall if he is to be counted as healthy.

Jack said, "Don't pay any attention to those numbers because they are averages. To arrive at the average, each lab samples the data for all of the people who have been tested. They eliminate the top 10% and the bottom 10% and then get an average number from the remaining 80%. Since the majority of people who get their blood tested have an ailment of some kind, it means that the remaining 80% from which the average is taken are people who are less than 100% healthy in the first place!

"Since the goal is to get you to optimal health, we are going to use optimal health ranges instead. That way you can work toward being totally healthy, not just equal to the average of the sample of unhealthy people."

This one medical example is symptomatic of human nature. In this case, you go to the doctor to see if you are healthy. But healthy compared to what? As long as you fit within the average of people in your age group, the doctor gives you a clean bill of health. Fall below average and the doctor gets on your case. Above average? The doctor congratulates you and says, "If you can keep it up, that is great," as if to say that you don't really need to change your habits if you don't want to because most people don't.

We are a culture committed to being average. Early on in our educational experience we get our first and most lasting lesson in being average. It comes when we are introduced to the grading system which in many cases is based on the Bell Curve. It works in much the same way as the blood test. It mandates that 10% will fail, 10% will be excellent, and the remaining 80% will be average. It automatically assumes and creates a big mass in the middle that is average.

Being good enough. Most high school students who come to Eagle "U" initially commit to get better grades. But when I ask them, as I always do, what exactly "better" means, their response usually implies that what they really want is to do as little as they can to keep Mom and Dad off their backs. They just want to do average which seems to be good enough to accomplish that.

But what about the bear trap? All things being left to themselves, human nature tends toward the comfortable. Goldilocks and the three bears were our first instructors in this philosophy:

* Not too hot and not too cold.
* Not too hard and not too soft.
* We're not happy until it's juuuuuuuuuust RIGHT!

So into the classroom we go. The classroom is the laboratory that provides regular, measurable feedback in the life of the young person. The first day of class, the high school teacher goes over the course requirements including required reading, regular assignments, and the schedule for exams. Occasionally the instructor will even talk about extra credit activities for those who are interested.

About 80% of the high school students in the average class spend a lot of time trying to discover what is the least amount of work they have to do to get by. The reason they do this lies in the answer to the question, "Who gets the most attention in school?"

* The excellent student?

* The average student?

* The failing student?

If you chose the failing student first and the excellent student second, you are right on.

The failing students get lots of negative reinforcement. Every time they get a poor grade, everyone is on their case--parents, teachers, counselors, coaches, etc.

The excellent students get some attention, although much less. Most of the attention they get is in the form of a few congratulations and a lot of pressure to keep up the great performance.

It is the average student who has it made in the shade as they say. They don't do poorly enough for anyone to get alarmed, but they don't do so well that they create what they think is unrealistic expectations from everyone for the future. Their performance is juuuuuuuuuuust RIGHT!

Because the entire system is designed to create one big mass of average performances in the middle, we all come to expect and accept just that--AVERAGE!

Consider the failure filter. Average parents listen through a filter or bias. Since they know that the teenage years are high risk for bad grades, bad friends, and bad habits, most parents listen to and watch for all of the initial signs of failure. Every action, every conversation, every interaction is processed through the are-there-any-signs-of-failure filter.

If the analysis comes out negative, meaning there are no signs of failure yet, then they are satisfied. In fact, most parents are so happy that their children are not in the failure category that they accept average performance with overwhelming gratitude. After all, things could be much worse!

Fear of failure is a much bigger motivator than desire for gain. Just test this one out on your teens sometime. Try to get them to go and pick up trash for 30 minutes on the local highway in exchange for five dollars. Most young people won't even budge an inch at the offer. Reach over and grab their wallet or purse, take five dollars out and walk away and see what happens! I'll guarantee they will have something to say about it. They'll fight to get back what rightfully belongs to them.

The moral is that we will fight to keep from losing what we have, but will think twice about exerting much effort to gain the same thing if we don't have it.

The same rule applies to the parents' inclination to motivate young people. It is much more natural to be fearful of their potential failure than to focus on their potential success. And so the majority of the communication can easily center around:

* Not failing.
* Staying out of trouble.
* Getting good grades (whatever those are).
* Not messing up.

In other words, doing just enough to get by is satisfactory--not too hot, not too cold. Juuuuuuuuuuust RIGHT!

Ask yourself if you have come to accept average?

1. Do you accept vague commitments from your young person such as, "I'll do better next time" or "I'll try harder?"

2. Are you guilty of giving more negative feedback when performance drops than you are of giving positive reinforcement when performance improves?

3. How fine-tuned is your failure filter? Are you continually listening for signs and signals of future failure and just being relieved when you see none?

4. How much are you motivated by the fear of failure? What percentage of your conversation is centered around staying out of trouble, doing better in school, or not messing up?

SOLUTION
Commit to Excellence

There is little satisfaction to be found in being average. It sometimes produces ease and comfort, but not personal satisfaction. Great personal satisfaction and confidence come from setting objectives, carrying out a plan, and reaching that objective. Once that exhilaration is felt, the ease and comfort of average performance dulls by comparison.

Teach by example. Like most solutions to the 13 biggest mistakes parents make, it all starts with your example. You can't teach something you don't do any more than you can go back to a place you've never been!

For ten years I have made an annual trip to New Braunfels, Texas, where I have a standing invitation to speak to all of the senior students from the three local high schools. As I do with all groups of students, I put them through an exercise to illustrate the power of goal setting.
I have all of the students stand up. I then ask them the following four questions. If they answer "no" to any one of these questions they are asked to sit down.

Question 1: "Do you have goals?" Most stay standing.

Question 2: "Are your goals written down?" About 50% sit down.

Question 3: "Do you review them every day?" That eliminates 90% of those remaining.

Question 4: "Do you have them written down and with you?" Two or three are left standing if we are lucky.

One year in New Braunfels, a scrappy looking African American young man was the only one left standing. As always I had the crowd applaud. I then asked him a few questions. He happened to be a state champion in track and had earned a full-ride college scholarship. He shared that he had set both of those goals several years back and had worked very hard to achieve them all during high school.

When I asked him who taught him to do this, he replied that it was his dad. He said, "I learned this when I was a little kid. My dad has done it every since I can remember and I just copied him."

A good example has motivating power that is much greater than multiple admonitions!

I was inspired by this young man's story. I was determined to do for my children what this boy's father had done for him--teach goal setting and a commitment to excellence by example. I had always set goals. It was something my dad showed me how to do at a young age and he demonstrated by his example as well. But I was not sure that my goals were visible enough in our own home. So I posted my goals on the bathroom mirror where I could see them and review them morning and night. They were visible to everyone in the family.

On several occasions over the next few weeks I came across one of our daughters who was in the first grade at the time reading over my goals. She even asked what they were.

What happened next was totally unexpected however. During a brief family outing one evening about a month later, this same daughter spoke up from the back seat of the car and reminded me that I had not taken her mother out on her date that week which is one of the goals I had listed on the mirror! While I was trying to teach her by the things I had hung on the mirror, she was watching the more important thing--my actions.

A commitment to excellence in the family starts at the top--with the head of the household. Young people will act more on what they see than on what they hear. **So ask yourself**:

* Do I have goals?

* Have I written them down?

* Do I review them every day?

* Do I carry a list of my goals with me and follow
  with daily actions to help me reach them?

If you are not doing these things, start NOW!

Excellence at any age. One of the greatest gifts young people can receive is the gift of a clear vision of their current and future potential. When they can't see it clearly at first, you can provide a looking glass through which they can see the map to their future potential.

Make a treasure map to success. Try this with a child or adult of just about any age. Collect a wide variety of magazines--business, sports, home and garden, outdoor, etc. Sit down with your young person with a pairs of scissors, some glue and a large sheet of posterboard for each of you. Explain that you are each going to go through the magazines and clip out pictures and phrases that represent things that you would like to **be, do,** and **have** in the future.

As you do your treasure map and your young person does his or hers, you can discuss what things you are each choosing and why they are important. You might want to make suggestions along the way regarding academic achievements, activities, career plans, family goals, etc. Let him/her see what you are doing and explain your choices and why they are important to you.

Arrange the pictures and phrases on the posterboard. When each of you is happy with the quantity and quality of the things you have chosen, you can glue them down. Have your young person hang this treasure map where it will be seen daily. Update it occasionally together. It can be the beginning of a life of setting and achieving goals.

Reinforce the goal setting habit. Each year at Eagle "U" we carefully select our faculty and mentors, including special guest speakers who change from year to year in order to give our returning students different perspectives and examples of pathways to success. One of our guest speakers has been Jeffrey Gitomer, author of *The Sales Bible* and *Customer Satisfaction is Worthless, Customer Loyalty is Priceless.* He suggests that each goal setter obtain a pad of sticky notes and write a different goal on each one. The goals are posted on the bathroom mirror for daily review and reinforcement. When each goal is accomplished it is moved to the bedroom mirror. Thus the bathroom mirror becomes the reflection of future success and the bedroom mirror becomes the reflection of accomplishment. Both mirrors become powerful reinforcement for excellence.

Maybe there is some value in going to the dogs. If you have ever trained a dog, you know one of the keys to behavior change is not to kick the dog or otherwise punish him when he does something wrong. Dogs can understand that they are getting attention but have difficulty differentiating between good and bad reward. So the more successful approach to training is to reward the behavior you want and ignore the behavior you don't want.

I am in no way suggesting that young people are dogs or are "going to the...," but there is a lesson to be learned from the training method. It is that if you reward the behavior you want, you are likely to get more of it.

When there is only the slightest improvement in average performance, it rarely gets rewarded and so the performance remains average. But like the example of puppy training, if improvement is acknowledged, recognized and rewarded, it is more likely to be repeated.

For example: Young Bob sets a goal to get better grades--to improve his grade point average from a "C" to a "B" or better. Your job is to watch every assignment. Congratulate him on the slightest improvement in each test score. Recognize every minor accomplishment. Don't wait for the final result. Most of us can't wait that long for feedback and reinforcement. We need it NOW! The closer the feedback and recognition is to the desirable action that created it, the more likely that action is to be repeated.

So catch your young people doing the right things. Recognize and acknowledge the initial minor improvements and you're likely to get more of them in the future. If after following this course, you still have a problem with unacceptable behavior, go back to the chapter titled *Mistake 4–Having a House With No "Walls"* for an appropriate remedy.

Replace the failure filter with a confidence coach. When goals are set and the vision is clear, the communication can take a whole new direction. Instead of listening and watching for every sign of slipping performance, you can now coach with confidence as you focus the majority of your conversation on the positive things that you and your young person want. The following changes can help:

Change comments about "not failing" **to** conversations about successful accomplishment of the goals that have been set and the steps necessary to reach them.

Change discussions about staying out of trouble **to** asking, "What did you do today to get closer to accomplishing your goal?"

Change emphasizing good grades (whatever those are) **to** recognizing the daily accomplishments that will lead toward specific goal accomplishment for an improved grade point average.

Change admonitions about not messing up **to** words of encouragement such as, "I know you can do it and make it happen!"

When you focus on what you want instead of what you don't want (or what you fear), your behavior, conversation, and the reinforcement will all align to move your young person in the right direction.

Keep Your Young Person from Becoming an Average Catfish by Creating a Commitment to Excellence

1. Lead by example: Have goals written down. Review them daily and carry them with you.

2. Create a treasure map with your young people to get them into the goal setting habit.

3. Reinforce their goals by using the sticky note system–goals to be accomplished on the bathroom mirror; goals that have been accomplished on the bedroom mirror.

4. Recognize and acknowledge each and every small initial improvement. Reward more of what you want and less of what you don't want.

5. Be a confidence coach. Center your conversation around encouraging goal accomplishment instead of fear of failure.

MISTAKE 7
Having a House Divided

"...every city or house divided against itself shall not stand."
(Matthew 12:25).

Many Eagle "U" students voluntarily share with us what their home environment is like, especially as it has to do with their relationship with their parents.   Guess who are the first ones to figure out when Mom and Dad aren't pulling together?

Here's a typical example of some of the things we hear from different teenagers we work with: (The names have been changed.)

Dave: "I always know who to go to when I want something. Dad has one answer for everything--'No.' Mom is the one who is the pushover. I can get her to give me anything."

Sara: "My parents fight so much that they hardly have time to see what is really going on in my life. If they only knew."

Ted: "My parents just don't see eye-to-eye on most things, so I just do whatever I want to do."

McKenzie: "We don't do much together as a family. We all just do our own thing."

Mark: "Rules? What rules? They change from day to day depending on who is running the show--Mom or Dad."

Peter: "Mom is definitely the one to avoid. She runs the show while Dad just hides."

Becky: "My parents got divorced five years ago when I was eleven. Dad is a blast. I love it when we are together. We have so much fun. I just dread having to go back to my mother. She's just too strict."

Ron: "My parents had a pretty bad divorce. They've each been trying ever since to get me and my two sisters to side with them. They don't have anything good to say about each other."

These are symptoms of a House Divided. Just as a well-built house starts with a firm foundation, secure, well-adjusted children get their initial sense of security from parents who have a good relationship with each other. When there is a division in any of a variety of ways, the sense of security that is so critically needed early in life begins to erode.

When security declines, so does self-confidence, beginning then and on into the future. Lack of self-confidence begins to show up in poor performance in school, lack of direction, and ultimately in the "catfish" behavior described in the opening chapter of this book.

Are there any of the following House Divided symptoms in your home or family relationships?

1. **Can't get it from one so they get it from the other:** Young people from the earliest age figure this one out in a hurry. If Mom says "No" then run to Dad and see if you can get the answer you want. When the troops sense that the generals are not united in philosophy, purpose, or response, they have no confidence in the leadership. With no clear leadership, there is little sense of security. With no security at home, they will start looking for it elsewhere.

2. **Disrespectful communication and resistance to direction.** Because we all learn most of what we do from example, the communication you sow is the communication you will reap later.

Sid's sad example: Sid's dad was very disrespectful of women. He could often be heard making derogatory comments about "the weaker sex." He treated his wife as inferior and frequently talked down to her. Since his father was his first and most prominent role model, Sid subconsciously adopted all of his father's attitudes toward women, including his mother, and took on all of his father's poor communication habits.

Carolyn's imitation: Carolyn's parents rarely agreed on anything. Since they were in conflict most of the time, their communication with each other was filled with anger and disrespect. How Carolyn's parents treated each other eventually became the pattern for the way Carolyn started treating her parents.

3. **Disagreements with no boundaries or rules.** It is likely that 100% of the family members are never going to agree with each other on 100% of the issues 100% of the time. Disagreement is not the problem. It's how you deal with it that creates the problem.

Boxing may be one of the more violent sports in our culture. But imagine a boxing match with no rules for a fair fight. Punch anywhere, anytime in any way you like. Gloves or no glove--do as you please! Such a match would only have one result--catastrophe.

In much the same way, any home that has not created the rules for dealing with and eventually resolving disagreements is in for catastrophic results--out of control behavior, unacceptable language, and hurt feelings resulting in mutual loss of respect. And when respect is gone, a sense of security goes right along with it.

4. **Disagreement over discipline or rules.** Any astute strategist knows that if you can get the leaders fighting with each other,

the empire will soon be at odds and nothing much will be accomplished.

Nothing is quite as confusing to a child or a young person as parents who can't agree on rules for discipline, argue about what is or is not appropriate for the children to do, and argue about it all in front of the kids. Few things create more insecurity in the hearts and minds of young people than parents who fight in front of them.

5. **The undermining parent:** Peter was raised by an overly strict father and an overly compensating mother. The dad insisted that the boy tow the line and be dependably self-disciplined. Dad told him exactly what the boundaries were financially, the chores he had to do, and the allowance he would receive, etc. Everything had a rule. This would seem to be in harmony with sound principles, but the way in which it was done was rather overbearing and oppressive.

A greater problem developed when the mother, who had a soft heart, was overly charitable with the boy. She responded to every little complaint Peter had. She would secretly give him cash every time he wanted to do something that would not be possible under the dad's allowance system.

When Peter went to college Dad still had the clear guidelines established and the son continued to call home with his sob stories to Mother who continued to send him extra money. Seven years into college he still had not graduated. When his dad finally cut off the college funds, Peter went to work but could not keep a job for more than six months. He had no direction, goals, or idea of where he was going, and especially no one to give him a financial subsidy when he was unproductive.

Peter paid a high price for parents who could not work together for his own good. To this day, Peter's dad has no idea why his son has turned out like he has.

6. The house divided by divorce. With over half of marriages ending in divorce, a majority of kids fall victim to a house divided by divorce. There are two common ailments in this situation:

    a. Different rules and discipline from each parent. One house is more fun than the other. Since Mom and Dad couldn't agree in marriage, they usually don't agree outside of it either. With no commonly held set of rules and boundaries, the young people flounder.

    b. "Side with me." Since the desire to be right is so strong, divorced parents often choose to make their former spouse wrong in front of the kids. The reasoning goes that "Somehow if I can look good to the kids and make my former spouse look bad, the kids will side with me and that will make me right." It is the children in this situation who end up paying the price for this sick and twisted logic.

How divided is your house?

Yes	No	
☐	☐	Do your young people regularly attempt to get from one parent what they can't get from the other?
☐	☐	Do you ever speak disrespectfully to your spouse, especially in front of your children?
☐	☐	Do you ever speak disrespectfully about your spouse at any time, but especially within earshot of your children?
☐	☐	Do you have disagreements at home with your spouse or children that get out of control because there are no rules for resolving conflicts?

		Do you have disagreements with your spouse about discipline or rules in front of the children?
☐	☐	Have you ever been guilty of going against discipline or rules that your spouse had imposed with one of your children behind your spouse's back?
☐	☐	Do you ever say derogatory things about your spouse to your children?
☐	☐	Are there any areas of discipline, rules, or appropriate behavior for your children with which you and your spouse or former spouse disagree that remain unresolved?

SOLUTION
Create a Unified Home

Over the last ten years I have taken a particular interest in the Eagle "U" students who seem to be self-confident and secure with themselves--those who seem to have all of the right tools to avoid the "catfish" catastrophe. What is the common denominator? Are they just born that way, or is there something going on at home that makes a difference?

While there are exceptions to every rule, there seems to be some consistency among the students who have it all together. Many of them come from a home that is solid and not divided. It starts with Mom and Dad.

So we went and talked to their parents to see what was going on behind the scenes. They shared with us some great tips and some of their own secrets for creating the right environment at home that provides a sense of security and confidence for everyone in it.

United Home Rule #1:
Partner first–children second

Most of the parents we talked to made it clear that their personal relationship with each other comes first and the children know it! In most cases, the kids weren't around when you started your family and they certainly aren't going to be around the house forever if you do your job right! The most secure students we've encountered have a high degree of confidence in their parents' relationship. They seem to know that their parents are in harmony on the issues that really matter. Here's how these parents communicate that principle regularly:

Greet your spouse immediately and preferably first. Every night upon arriving home, most of the parents we talked to told us they make it a point to warmly greet their spouse first before anyone else at home. And it goes way beyond a "Hi honey, I'm home" greeting. It includes a quality hug and a happy greeting. Done daily, this sends the message that all is well with the leadership at home.

Daily, uninterrupted communication time. Many parents have made it a habit to have communication time together as soon as they arrive home. The children, no matter the age, are trained that this time is for Mom and Dad--no interruptions and no exceptions. Even if it just lasts ten minutes, it allows the two of you to get on the same page together. More importantly, it communicates to the family that you consider each other your most important priority.

Date night. My own parents were the best at this. Friday nights with frequent regularity would find Mom and Dad out doing something together. Whether it was a play, a movie or going shopping together, we always saw them going off to do things that they seemed to enjoy--together. Mom and Dad have always been great friends. The quality of their relationship is even more apparent today now that all of the kids are gone. Now they are on a twenty-four-hours-a-day, seven-days-a-week date and seem to enjoy it more than ever! But during our growing-up years, they gave all of us a great sense of security through making each other a priority and showing it.

Loyalty. You'll remember back when I talked about my father's response the first time he heard me say "no" to my mother: "You don't say "no" to your mother."

There was never any question about whose side Dad was on or whose side Mom was on. We always knew they were on the same team, playing out of the same "playbook." In those occasional situations where there may have been some disagreement between me and one of them, they always stuck together to support each other and back each other up. It was pretty useless even thinking about trying to get from one what I couldn't get from the other. Besides the fact that we were not allowed to even attempt it, it would have been a useless waste of time!

The greatest gift: There are some vivid and pointed experiences in my own life when Dad shared some really important wisdom with me. One of those was the day he told me, **"The greatest gift you can give your future children is to love their mother."**

Although he told that to me as a teenager some twelve plus years before I would marry, it is a rule I have never forgotten. The greatest gift he has given each of his seven children is exactly that. We've always known that Dad loves Mom and Mom loves Dad because they have always made each other the priority. It has given all of us a great sense of security as a result.

United Home Rule #2:
Create your own family constitution

Being the last of seven children has several advantages, one of which is benefitting from the experience of my older brothers and sisters who have gone through just about everything in life before I have.

When I was a senior in high school, one of my older sisters got engaged. Things were pretty exciting around our house as wedding plans were made. One evening, she and her fiancé decided to stay at our house for their date as they worked together discussing, defining and writing down the family values they were going to subscribe to. I don't remember what was on the list, but the fact that they would go through that process was impressive and something that I did with my future wife before we got married.

The greatest gift the Founding Fathers gave the United States of America was the Constitution. It not only contains a great organizational plan of government, but also the core beliefs and values that are the foundation of that organization. Every young person would benefit from being part of a family that took the time to define their most important values. Great confidence and self-assurance comes from learning and understanding

- mutual respect
- trust
- dependability
- courtesy
- kindness
- cleanliness

and many other potential family values. Where else are young people going to learn about what matters most? If it doesn't happen at home, it is not likely that it ever will happen.

It's never too late to start on your own family constitution. If you have teenagers at home, do it together. Discuss, define and write down the values that matter most to your family. Hang it on the wall. Review it together often.

United Home Rule #3:
Decide what's a fair fight!

Most of us aren't really good at resolving conflict. Unless you have received some specific training in this area, you will usually resort to what comes naturally–emotional reaction! Part of having a united home is deciding in advance how you are going to handle disagreements. Here are some examples you might want to consider:

A. **Discuss in private first:** Initially discuss rules, discipline and consequences for your young people privately with your spouse before talking about it with your children. Come to an agreement on the core issues. If you can't agree on a specific issue, get some counseling or agree in advance on someone such as a religious leader or a mentor you both look up to who can give you some advice and counsel. Young people get a lot of benefit from parents who are united on the most important issues in their life.

B. **Have a way to signal time out:** Agree in advance on some type of a signal you can give your spouse if something comes up over which you disagree that has to do with your children. That signal means "time out." You are going to go do some work with each other before you involve the child.

C. **Establish some communication rules:** When working through a disagreement with your spouse, take personal responsibility for your own emotions without placing blame. Use "I" statements to describe how and why you feel the way you do. For example:

> Wrong way: "You made me so mad when you let Johnny off so easy."

> **Right way:** "I felt very upset when I found out you

told him he could leave with his friends after I told him yesterday that he could not go."

Wrong way: "You never listen to what I think is important for her. It's always your way and that's it."

Right way: "I really get aggravated when we don't take the time to discuss and agree in advance what is best for her. I feel as if I don't have any say."

Wrong way: "You never listen. It's no wonder she turns you off."

Right way: "I feel bad for her when she is in the middle of saying something important and you interrupt her and tell her what she has to do. I can see the resentment all over her face when that happens."

The young people we deal with at Eagle "U" who have the best communication skills and who know how to resolve conflict learned it at home from the example of their parents. Work on the communication skills with your spouse first, and your children will eventually see your example and learn the appropriate way to work out disagreements.

D. **Use the one to ten system:** In areas of disagreement with your spouse or the kids that are not values related and don't have serious moral consequences, an honest 1 to 10 rating system is a useful way to move things along. Here is a simple example:

You are on your way to see a movie together with your spouse. Your spouse has been waiting to see a particular movie ever since it came out. You don't have much interest in it and would rather see something else. It's decision time. The question might be to say to your spouse, "On a scale of one to ten, how much do you really want to see this movie?" For your spouse, it might be an eight. For you, the movie is about a two! So off you go to the movie and you are happy about it!

If on those rare occasions when going or doing something is a ten for one of you and not going or doing it is a ten for the other, take turns going along with the other person's choice.

E. The solution of final resort: Every well run organization has a system set up for final decisions if agreement can't be reached. If the executives in a corporation can't agree on a course of action, it's the C.E.O.'s job to make the decision. While everyone may not agree with the decision once it has been made, it does become their responsibility to follow through.

Just like any well-organized group, every family needs a leader, the person who makes the final decision on those rare occasions when a decision has to be made and there is no consensus.

Growing up, there was never any question about who the final authority was in our family. Dad was the head of the house. That's because Mom and Dad clearly understood and agreed on that together. It is how the home was organized. On those few occasions when Dad had to make the decision, Mom was always 100% behind him and we all knew it. Even though we may not have agreed with his decision, it provided all of us with a high degree of confidence and security knowing that Mom supported Dad even when she may not have agreed at the moment either.

Learning how to properly disagree and resolve conflict is one of the most powerful things you can do to create a united home. It is one of the greatest gifts you can give your children by your own example.

United Home Rules for the House that Has Already Been Divided

Making the best of divorce. With over half of marriages ending in divorce, at least half or more of the young people we work with at Eagle "U" come from family situations where Mom and Dad are no longer together. Here is a brief list of ideas from divorced parents who have worked hard to stay focused on the development of their children in the face of the challenges that divorce gives:

- ❑ **Make the success of your young person a priority.** Although you may not agree on very many things with your former spouse, do whatever you have to do to agree on one fundamental principle–that the success and well-being of your young person is going to be a priority for both of you, and you are going to do what you have to do to make that happen.

- ❑ **Get a mentor.** Appoint, if necessary, a third party that both you and your former spouse trust who will serve as the person who can make final decisions about what to do on those occasions when you and your former spouse may not agree on what to do with or for your young person. It might be a godparent, a religious leader or other mentor who has the child's best interests at heart. It has to be someone you both trust–someone with whom you both make an agreement that you will abide by his or her decisions.

- ❑ **Set up clear rules and consequences for your young person** that both you and your former spouse will enforce. Nothing is more confusing to a child of any age than parents who are not consistent. If one parent's rules are different than other parent's, everyone loses.

❑ **Decide what you will and will not give your young person.** Parents who try to out do each other by giving the child more or better gifts or allowing the child to have more freedoms than the other parent only damages the future success of the young person.

❑ **Never say anything disrespectful or negative about your former spouse in front of your young person.** Regardless of how you may feel, your former spouse is still your child's parent. Too many young people we have worked with assume that they have the same shortcomings or weaknesses as one parent accuses the other of having. That is to say that if something is perceived to be wrong with Mom or Dad, the young person often thinks the same thing, or something equally bad, is wrong with him/her. Unfortunately it is the highest price that many children pay for a "house divided." It is a price that many of them pay for a lifetime in terms of low self-esteem and a low self-image that is never totally reversed.

The Ultimate Goal of a United Home

My wife, Cheryl, comes from a less than ideal background, having been raised with all of the liabilities that come from a house divided and then some. Having been in and out of more foster homes as a young child than she cares to remember, one of her stated goals when we were engaged to be married was that she wanted to give our future children something she had never received as a child--an emotionally and physically safe united home.

One evening, several months after we were married, I returned home from work to find her sitting on the living room floor of our little starter home sobbing. I immediately sat down next to her and asked her what had happened. With tears rolling down her face she said, "When I came home tonight and walked through the door, I had the distinct feeling for the first time in my life that

I was finally <u>home</u>." Then I started crying right along with her!

Over the years that have followed, I watch in amazement as she gives to our children something she never received as a child--the gift of emotional, spiritual, and physical safety in a united home. She does it in an extraordinary way.

The greatest gift children can receive from parents is not a big house, getting their own car when they are sixteen or getting lots of <u>stuff</u> for every birthday and holiday. The greatest gift they can receive is at the hands of loving parents who love each other first and stick together to create a united home environment in which each child can grow and develop with a sense of emotional security. Nothing money can buy will replace that.

The United Home Builder's Checklist

1. **Partner first, children second**: Make your marriage the priority. Let your children see, hear and feel that your relationship with your spouse is the most important one in your life. Great security, confidence and self-esteem come to the young person whose parents are united and show it daily. Remember: the greatest gift you can give your young person is to love your spouse.

2. **Create your own family constitution.** Write down and define the values that matter to you most as a family. Hang it up where everyone can see it. Review it together often.

3. **Decide today how you will handle disagreements tomorrow:**

   - Agree to discuss disagreements about the children privately first with your spouse.

   - Decide how you will signal "time out" for decision

making.

- Work on and practice your rules for communication in conflict such as using "I" statements.

- Use the one to ten system for family decision making on less serious matters.

- Understand who the leader of the family is, especially on those occasions when you need a final decision.

4. Follow united home rules even if you are divorced:

- Make the success of your young person a priority.

- Get a mentor.

- Set up clear rules and consequences for your young person that both you and your former spouse will enforce.

- Never say anything disrespectful or negative about your former spouse in front of your young person.

MISTAKE 8
Failing to Understand and Act on
the Feather Philosophy

If I were to have a one-on-one conversation with you about your young person right now, especially if he or she is a teenager, one of the first questions I would ask would be this:

Tell me about his/her friends:

- What are they like?
- What do they do in their spare time?
- Are they high achievers?
- Do they get good grades?
- Are they self-motivated?
- Do they have goals and if so, what are they?

In some ways, I would want to know more about your young person's friends than I initially would want to know about your young person. Why?

Because birds of a feather flock together. It is a powerful natural law. We call it the **Feather Philosophy.**

If you were to see a large flock of geese, you would never expect to see a duck, raven, hawk or pelican flying in that same flock It's just not natural. It doesn't happen. Animals naturally seek their own kind. And so do people!

Walk into just about any high school, the great microcosm of the social and psychological world, and you'll see it in action:

- The jocks hang out with other jocks.
- The nerds hang out with other nerds.

- The cheerleaders hang out with other cheerleaders.

Exceptions to this rule are rare. When they occur, everyone notices! But in general, like attracts like. We tend to gravitate to those who are like us. That is why the truth of the age-old saying starts to manifest itself at an early age: **The measure of a man** (a woman or a young person) **is the company he keeps.** But have you also considered that the opposite is also true? **The company he keeps can determine the measure of the man?**

Ice or water? If you put ice cubes in room temperature water, the ice soon changes form and becomes water. But if you put the resulting water in the freezer compartment of your refrigerator, it will soon change back into ice. Matter naturally adjusts to the temperature of the environment around it. People are the same way in terms of their attitudes and beliefs. This is especially true of young people.

In our own work with high school students across the country, we have found that what their friends do is the single biggest factor that determines:

- the school activities they participate in,
- whether or not they choose to go to college,
- and where they go to college if they choose to go.

I'm sure it is no news flash to you that the closer your young people approach the teenage years, the more your natural influence dwindles and the natural influence of their friends strengthens.

They tend to adopt the
- attitudes,
- beliefs,
- habits and
- characteristics
of their friends whom they
- spend the most time with,
- appear to be the most accepted by,
- think are the most popular,

- feel most comfortable with, and
- allow to have the most influence on them.

You see, not only do birds of a feather flock together, but **flocking causes birds to be of the same feather!**

A naturally high achieving 16 year-old young man came to Eagle "U." His parents had decided early on to home school him and his sister. The learning environment they provided for their children made them thirst for knowledge. They studied rigorously and became outstanding students.

When the boy reached high school age, the parents decided that it would be nice for him to be able to participate in the extracurricular activities at the local high school. So together, parents and son decided to enroll him in the public high school.

For the first few weeks he really poured it on. He asked a lot of questions in class and did his assignments with an eye on perfection just as he had always done at home. Things seemed to be working quite well for him in the new school.

Then gradually, almost imperceptibly at first, he began studying less. His desire to do extra credit assignments tapered off. He participated less in class. And then his grades dropped. What was happening?

After some long discussions between the parents and the son, he admitted that things started out well in the new school, but that the other boys began giving him a hard time about "sucking up to the teacher." Since it wasn't "cool" in this school to be smart, he gradually, even subconsciously, began adopting the attitudes about school that the most socially "in" students seemed to have. He didn't realize that his delinquent and less capable friends were just trying to drag him down to their level. **People tend to take on the characteristics of the dominating or most powerful influence around them.**

Most parents want an answer to the question, "What do you do about it?" Here are some suggestions straight from the home of the Feather Philosophy, Eagle "U." After all, we even named it after this most famous high flying bird!

SOLUTION
Obey the Natural Laws of the Feather Philosophy

Natural laws are powerful forces. So powerful, in fact, that it is very difficult to overcome them:

• You can't defy gravity without millions of dollars of equipment and fuel to get you off the ground and keep you there.

• It requires layers of warm clothing and protection to keep you from freezing to death in below zero weather.

• You can't prevent a naturally occurring chemical reaction unless you keep the chemicals separated from each other.

In other words, you just can't fool mother nature! So instead of fighting what naturally occurs in nature, start working with it. Put the following natural laws to work for you.

Law #1
Water seeks its own level

Go ahead. Fill up the bathtub and then really stir things up. Get the water sloshing back and forth, splashing up one side and then the other. Then stand back and wait. Watch. What happens? Gradually the water settles down and eventually comes to rest on an even plain, all at the same level.

In much the same way as the water, we all want to level off with the majority where we feel most comfortable. Young people do the same thing. They tend to gravitate, settle in, and settle down with the people and the friends with whom they feel most comfortable.

So what can you do about that? A lot!

To change the water level, add more water! If you want the water in that tub to rest at a higher level, just put more water in the tub! If you want your young people to seek a higher level of friends, you have to go to work on their self-image.

How I see myself determines the people with whom I choose to surround myself. It's simple cause and effect:

- Lousy self-image--lousy friends.

- High self-image--high caliber friends.

- Poor self-image as a student--friends who are poor students.

- High self-image as an athlete--friends who are great athletes.

- Great self-image as a leader--friends who are self-directed.

- Great self-image as a future success--friends who have success habits.

To change young people, change their self-image and they will change their environment and the people with whom they choose to associate.

What you see is what you get. Go and watch a small infant and you will witness self-image in the making by imitation. Early on, we learn almost all of what we do by copying those around us. The infant copies or imitates the facial expressions, sounds and movements of his or her primary caregiver.

We may grow older, but we don't change the pattern. In fact, we are more than half of what we are by imitation. Help your young people choose good models because they will naturally copy those with whom they associate. Create opportunities for them to associate with "eagles."

Flocking with Eagles. One of the inspirations for Eagle "U" came from an early experience I had as a young teenager that had a powerful influence on my self-image.

Since my dad was in advertising, he helped promote an annual Success Rally where all of the greatest speakers in the country would come and present for three days. Business people and professionals would pack the house to hear the likes of Art Linkletter, Zig Ziglar, Paul Harvey and others.

Each year Dad would give me an opportunity to attend. Sometimes we would go together and other times I would go alone. But I will never forget the distinct impression at one point of riding my bicycle to the local university's basketball facility where the rally was being held. As I locked my bike up outside and walked in, I noticed the other people around me, how they dressed, how they acted, and how they interacted. It gave me a clear picture of what was to come in my future adult life. It gave me a powerful image of what I would be like.

As I sat there, the environment, the things I saw and the things I heard had a powerful impact on me. As I left, I walked a little taller and thought a lot differently because the whole experience had positively influenced the image I had of myself at that point in my life and in the future.

Because of that experience, I have always wanted to give young people the same image altering experience by creating a success environment like we do at Eagle "U." I am always amazed at how young people see themselves a little differently when they get in an environment of "eagles." Then they go home, taking a piece of that environment with them, and start creating it in their own lives.

When they see themselves differently:

- Their self-image improves.
- They choose better environments in which to spend their time.
- Their choice of friends improves.
- They spend their time in more productive pursuits.
- They set out to accomplish more challenging things.

Change their self-image and they'll upgrade their friends.
Tom came to Eagle "U" between his sophomore and junior years of high school. He showed a lot of promise as a football player on his high school team.

When he returned home from Eagle "U," he resigned from the football team which was a shock to his parents and to all of us. When questioned about his decision, he told his parents that he had started to see himself a little differently after his experience at Eagle "U." And when he started looking around at his teammates, he could not find any one of them whom he admired, looked up to or wanted to be like. In short, he did not want to become like the other players with whom he was "flocking"on the team.

It was a drastic move and one that took a lot of courage, but one that paid off very shortly.

Early in the next season, some off the field events transpired involving the players on the football team that led to a police investigation, school suspension and criminal charges being brought against the players. The players on the team that year paid a heavy price for their involvement with each other in terms of damaged scholastic performance, a criminal record and a damaged reputation.

By acting on the feather philosophy--that you tend to become like the people with whom you associate--Tom saved himself a lot of unnecessary hassle and perhaps some life-long negative consequences. But it all started with an upgrade in his self-image which was already pretty good. When his self-image changed because of the positive environment he experienced at Eagle "U," he chose to change his own environment and the friends with whom he spent the most time.

Mentors. One of the most powerful experiences young people have at Eagle "U" is the mentor session where they have an opportunity to talk with successful people in a variety of fields who share with them their secrets of success. As the students ask, listen and learn, the image they have of themselves and the vision of what is possible in their future is dramatically improved. And when those internal pictures improve, so does the environment they choose to create for themselves when they return home, the friends they choose, the goals they set and how they spend their time.

Help your young people develop meaningful mentor relationships by:
- Understanding what their natural interests are.

- Identifying outstanding people in the areas of their natural interests.

- Finding ways they can associate with those people by observation and/or conversation.

Observation leads to imitation. Our local gymnastics coach is a big believer in changing self-image by observing mentors. She puts all of her future star performers on a steady diet of:

- Watching Olympic gold medal performances on video.
- Attending gymnastics competitions where older, successful athletes can be observed.
- Reading the success stories of championship competitors.

Feather philosophy action #1:

(a) Provide regular opportunities for your young people to be in environments where there are "eagles" they can observe and watch. Their self-image will be influenced accordingly.

(b) Identify mentors in areas where your young people have natural interests. Find ways to expose them to those mentors even if it is just observing what they do or reading about their lives. It will positively influence their own self-image and ultimately affect the choice of people with whom they choose to associate.

Law #2
Proximity determines influence

If you were going to cook dinner tonight and wanted to grill some fresh fish, you would naturally need to expose that fish to the direct heat of the stove or grill. If the stove were at one end of the kitchen and you stood at the other end with the fish, the fish would rot before it would ever cook. It has to be close to the source of the heat.

Young people are the same. If you want to continue having a positive influence in their lives as they grow, you have to stay close and involved.

Who moved first, the fish or the fire? I was talking with a father who was a successful entrepreneur and who was sending his son to Eagle "U." The sixteen year-old son was generally on a good track, got good grades and was active in school groups. Dad was concerned about some of his recent activities which included a girlfriend with whom he seemed to be spending a lot of time. His grades were slipping as a result.

In an effort to really understand the situation, I started asking some pointed questions:

Me: Tell me about his girlfriend. What is her name, what is she like, and what is she interested in?

Dad: I can't remember her name. She's only been to the house once. I don't know that much about her.

Me: What does your son like about her?

Dad: I don't really know. I've never really talked with him about it.

Me: What do they like to do most together when they go out?

Dad: I don't know. They're just always gone.

At that point I stopped. I knew exactly where the problem was. In this case, the son (the fish) had a new "flame" in many ways because Dad's "fire" had gone out! This father did not have a clue what was going on. He had no influence with his son because they weren't close. He wasn't involved as an active participant in his son's life. He was nothing more than a distant spectator.

Taking the fire to the fish. As a sophomore in high school I was on the sophomore football team. Most of my close friends were on the team. As a group we were focused and had high aspirations to go far. In many ways the team consisted of what I would consider a group of "eagles." We loved the game and we loved to play it together.

Meanwhile, back in the classroom, most of us on the team had ended up in the same history class taught by Mr. Jenkins. He took his job very seriously, and he definitely loved his subject a lot more than we did! Initially, most of us went through the motions of going to his class, studying enough to get a decent grade, and then moving on to the other things we had to do.

What we didn't know is that he expected more and wanted more from us. He not only wanted us to learn the subject, he wanted us to love it, internalize it, and make our future lives benefit from the lessons history has taught us.

Every Friday during football season when we went to Mr. Jenkins class, he would start by commenting about the game the afternoon before. He would specifically comment on the performance of particular members of the class. He would even ask us to comment on things that had transpired. Initially we thought it was nice, but little did we know the impact that was still to come.

Mid-season we had a football game in a city about an hour and a half from our school. Since the game was on a Thursday afternoon, few parents could attend. And since most of the students our age were not yet 16 years-old, few of them could drive to the game.

We traveled on the school bus to the opposing team's field. As we began the game, our bleachers were completely empty, while the other team had quite a cheering section. Midway through the second quarter we all noticed one person who had shown up to watch and cheer for our team. He sat all alone in the bleachers. It was Mr. Jenkins. We could not believe it. We never forgot it.

I can't remember whether we won or lost the game that day, but I do remember that it was the day the subject of history took on a whole new meaning and importance for all of us. Because he was interested and involved in our lives outside the classroom, Mr. Jenkins commanded respect, attention and great admiration from all of us in the classroom.

We would all do well to do the same with the young people in our lives–show an interest in what they are interested in.

Feather philosophy action #2: Stay close and stay involved with your young people every step of the way. Understand their interests. Get to know their friends. Know how they spend their time and what they enjoy doing. Stay proximate and you will continue to be influential in their lives.

Law #3
Nature always fills a vacuum

Remember one of those first simple physics experiments you did with the empty Coke bottle and a pealed hard-boiled egg? When you dropped a burning match in the empty Coke bottle and then placed the egg over the opening, what happened? As the burning match consumed all of the available oxygen in the bottle, the resulting vacuum sucked the egg down into the bottle.

There is a vacuum in all of us that seeks to be filled by a listening ear, an understanding heart and a nonjudgmental attitude. That vacuum is HUGE in young people. Since nature always works to fill a vacuum, who will fill it in your young person, you or someone else?

The mom who filled the vacuum. Craig was the oldest of four children and a junior in high school. He was a good student, very active in extracurricular activities, and very much on the right track. Before he came to Eagle "U" his mother explained to me everything that was going on in Craig's life in detail.

- She knew his fears.
- She understood his struggles.
- She knew what his goals were.
- She was plugged into his aspirations.
- She knew exactly how he felt about his girlfriend.
- She knew how he felt about each of his friends.
- She knew what subjects he liked best in school and which teachers he connected with.

In short, she knew just about everything about Craig. I naturally asked her how she did it. How did she get so close to her son?

She replied by asking me a few questions!

"Steve, think about the best friend you have ever had in your life; the one to whom you could tell anything; the one to whom you wanted to tell everything. When you have that person in mind, tell me the first characteristics that come to mind that made you so willing to open up and share everything with him."

I immediately thought of a best friend whom I had been very close to for many years. As I thought of that person, the first characteristics that popped into my mind were:

- concerned,
- understanding,
- nonjudgmental and
- a good listener.

When I shared those characteristics with her, she said: "I think you will find that Craig will use some of those same words to describe the relationship he has with me, his mother. Growing up is not easy and every young person seeks out someone to confide in. I just made a decision early that I was going to be the one that my children confided in. I have worked for years to develop those characteristics so I would be the one they sought out first."

How to make that happen would probably take an entire book in itself. But here are some communication habits to develop in order to start filling the natural vacuum that is waiting to be filled in every young person:

* Be interested. Show interest in what they are interested in whether you enjoy it or not! Be there. Be attentive. Be interested.

* Stop and listen. When was the last time you really had someone who listened to you when they weren't doing something else while you were talking, when they were totally focused on you and what you were saying? If you are like most people, it has been a while. So when was the last time you really sat down and listened to your young people? No distractions and no interruptions. Sometimes it has to happen on their terms and on their timetable. When they're ready, drop everything and listen up!

* Quit evaluating and start understanding. John just got dumped by his girlfriend. He is pretty down about it. His well-meaning father gives him a pep talk: "Don't worry son, she's not the only girl in the world. You'll get over it." John, however, doesn't need a pep talk, he needs an understanding ear. So quit telling and start ASKING, "How are you feeling about what happened?" Then just be quiet and listen. If they don't want to open up, that's OK. Just let them know that you are there whenever they want to talk.

* Make time to connect. Set aside the time on a regular basis to connect and communicate. The greatest missed opportunity today for most families is gathering around the dinner table each night, eating together and talking together. Family time is a must for connecting whether it is dinner or breakfast together, a specific night set aside each week to get together as a family, or a bedtime ritual where you spend ten or fifteen minutes together to debrief the day and make the time to connect. It is not going to happen by accident.

Feather philosophy action #3: Be the person in your young people's lives who fills their need to connect and communicate. Nature abhors a vacuum. Be the one to fill the void.

Law #4
Magnetized forces attract; polarized forces repel

Take two magnets and place the magnetized ends close together and they will attract. Turn the magnets around with the polarized ends facing each other and they repel.

People are just like magnets. We are naturally attracted to the environments that are compatible. They are the environments where we want to be. Most of the Eagle "U" students we work with who have maintained a close relationship with their parents have done so because their parents "magnetized" home and family by looking for ways to make it a desirable place for their young people to be.

These parents understand that **as children move into teenage life, parents compete with their friends for attention.** If parents don't make home and family a magnet with creative and fun things to do together, teenagers will flock to other places where someone else has control over the environment.

Here's how to be a magnet: Give them something to flock to! Friends of ours have done a great job of successfully navigating through the teenage years with their children and staying very close to them in the process. How did they do it? One way was with a boat! Most Fridays, as soon as everyone was home, the family was off to a local lake to water ski together. Frequently the children would take turns bringing a friend. There were strings attached to the outings: chores needed to be done first, and grades had to be maintained. The trips had to be earned. But Dad knew things were on track when most Friday afternoons his teenage boy was waiting in the driveway for him when he got home! Meanwhile, most other boys his age were hanging out with friends doing who knows what.

Snow birds. When I was about twelve, my dad decided that it was a crime to live near some of the most popular ski resorts in the world and not know how to ski! So we got some ski gear, enrolled in a ski class together and then spent nearly every winter Saturday morning skiing together. It was great bonding time for the two of us as we rode the ski lifts together and talked each week.

Make your home the nest they flock to. It was early on New Year's Eve day and I was at a local warehouse grocery store gearing up to have all of our Eagle "U" team leaders to our house before the start of our January session of Eagle "U." I bumped into our neighbors who have a high school age daughter who is a great student, very active in school, has "eagle" friends, and is very popular, especially with the boys! Their house was going to be party central that night for their daughter and her friends. They make it a point to make their home the place to be so they can interact with her friends and stay plugged into what is going on in her life. Over protective? Not really. Just involved.

Feather philosophy action #4: Work at developing things your young person will want to do with you and the family. Make home and family the cool place to be!

Law #5
Matter, over time, gravitates to its most disorganized state

This is called entropy and is a well-known law of physics. Just take a look at your garage, your clothes closet, or your junk drawer for examples of this law in action!

Our lives, especially young people's lives, tend to be the same. Without proper attention, life tends to get disorganized, chaotic and undisciplined.

Parents of Eagle "U" students who understand this natural law know that without some discipline in the system, young people can tend to gravitate to disorganized activities with no real purpose. Trouble emerges when everyone is just hanging out. So these parents have learned to control "entropy" with accountability.

So what's the plan? On a school related trip out of town, a teenage girl struck up an acquaintance with a young man from another city. A few weeks later the young man drove a considerable distance to see his new found friend.

As the young man and the girl contemplated leaving in the boy's car, the girl's father asked where they were going, what they planned to do, and when they would be back. The boy answered that he wasn't sure. He just thought they would kind of drive around, hang out and see what there was to do. The father responded, "At our house we always have a plan for what we are going to do, where we are going to do it, and when we will be back. Now I would like the two of you to just stay right here in the living room and talk. Until you have a plan for an approved activity and know when you'll be back, the living room will be a great place to hang out."

The daughter knew what the family standard was. It had been set long before. She didn't consider her father's comments heavy handed because the boundaries for accountability had been set up early on.

Too much, too little, or just right? A group of Eagle "U" students, young men in this case, were assembled at a break discussing the nature of their respective parents' rules for accountability:

Mike: "My parents always know where everyone in the family is and what they are doing. We have to let them know what's going on and who we are going to be with. They stay very involved in my life."

Scott: "Don't they trust you?"

Mike: "I feel like they believe in me and care enough to want to stay plugged into everything I am doing."

Darren: "I don't think my parents could care less about what is happening half the time in my life. I come and go as I please. They've got no clue what is going on in my life."

Ron: "You're a lucky dude. My parents drive me nuts. They're all over me all the time. They've got to know where I'm going, who I'm going to be with, and what we're going to be doing. It's like they think the moment I'm gone, I'm going to get into trouble. Half the time I just make stuff up to keep them happy."

What would your young person say about how you have set up the rules for accountability in your home?

- **Too much**; they want to push back.
- **Too little**; they may "flock" with the wrong kind of "birds" who they think care more about them than you do.
- **Just right**; they understand that you're involved because you care.

Feather philosophy action #5: Keep "entropy" in check with accountability. When you really care, you care to know what the plan is.

The Five Feather Philosophy Actions in Review

1. Work on the water level (self-image) and your young people will flock with eagles. Find environments where they can be with other "eagles." Find mentors with whom they share interests whom they can observe and emulate.

2. Stay proximate so as to stay influential in their lives: Be interested in what your children are interested in. Get to know their friends. Know how they spend their time and what they enjoy doing.

3. Fill the vacuum: Be the interested person in your young people's lives. Be the one who fills their need to connect and communicate.

4. Create the magnet your children are attracted to. Make home and family the cool place to be!

5. Keep "entropy" in check with accountability. When you really care, you care to know what the plan is.

MISTAKE 9
Providing Dependable "911 Emergency Rescue"

If you have ever lived in a small rural town, nothing signals your arrival into the real world like the implementation of the 911 emergency response system. We experienced that a few years ago while living in a small south central Texas town. The process involved much more than just providing an emergency phone number. Street names had to be checked for duplication and some names had to be changed. House numbers had to be verified and displayed prominently so that in case of an emergency, help would be sent to the right house. Finally, when all of the details were taken care of, the system was implemented. It gave all of the citizens in town a new sense of security, knowing help was just three digits away.

The success of any emergency system is dependent primarily on two things:

1. Competent professionals who know how to properly respond to emergency requests for help.

2. Citizens who exercise good judgment as to when to use the system.

Imagine a citizenry who starts using the 911 emergency response system for everyday needs such as asking for directions to someone's house because it's quicker than trying to find a city map; asking for someone's phone number since 911 has all the numbers; or asking about where to eat out because the emergency system has a listing for every restaurant in town.

Using the 911 system in this way would not only be socially irresponsible, it would not be tolerated. But if it were tolerated and accepted, many people would probably find it to be a great convenience and would use it frequently.

One of the many roles we all play as parents is that of an emergency response system. We're not only there to protect and defend, but to respond in case of dire emergency. Let's face it, growing up is tough sometimes. It is easy to screw up. Fortunately, if Mom and Dad are doing their job, emergencies can be minimized and tragedies averted. But when they can't, hopefully the same two people are there to care for, watch over, and look out for the best interests of an inexperienced child.

But what happens when there is a breakdown in the system and young people start using the emergency response system as if it were room service, and parents respond to every little request for help the same way as if it were a legitimate emergency?

The result is young people who:
- become overly dependent on parental "bail out,"
- learn little from their mistakes,
- lack a certain degree of personal responsibility, and
- ultimately never learn the skills to solve their own problems.

When help is always right around the corner, young people rarely learn how to assume personal responsibility. When there is always someone there to help solve every little problem, it becomes much easier to be a "catfish" because someone will always be there to get things back on track.

The abuse of the "911 emergency rescue system" takes on several forms. See if you are guilty of responding to any of them.

Abuse #1:   Calling 911-- "Comfort me when I quit."

Music has always been a big part of our lives and so all of the children in our family start taking piano lessons by the time they turn five. While shopping for a new piano at a local music store recently, a woman pulled us aside and said, "I couldn't help but overhear that you are looking for a new piano. If you want a really good deal, I would love to sell you ours. My daughter started piano last year but decided she did not like it. Now she's taking guitar so we don't need the piano. In fact, we don't need her flute or violin either. She started those, too, but decided she didn't like them. Hopefully she will stick with the guitar. This is getting expensive."

At what point will this girl learn persistence, determination, and follow through? Not until her mother stops rescuing her every time she quits, and stops paying out more money so she can try the next musical flavor of the week.

The comfort-me-when-I-quit problem often occurs in connection with college. The average college student today takes six years to complete what was originally designed to be a four-year curriculum. Why? Is it because the classes are harder or there are more graduation requirements? No! It is simply because too many college students can't make a decision about their major and when they finally do, they don't stick with it long enough to finish. When they change majors, the graduation requirements change and that prolongs their education. In the background are parents who are much too willing to continue paying the bills while the "catfish" swims through college with no direction and no commitment to a course of study.

An example of a drop-out's dream. Rick is a college student who has been raised by parents who have always been the "911 to the rescue" type. He finds college to be a little more challenging than he thought. He is not enjoying it, so he decides to quit like he as done so many times in other pursuits. He moves back home where someone else will provide for his every need, or more accurately, his every want. There is no urgency in his mind to make some progress towards becoming educated and getting started on a career path.

He lounges around the house for months while looking for just the right job. He gets a job and then quits because the boss isn't fair to him or he doesn't like what the job requires of him. He always has what in his mind is a good reason. Since there is no consequence to his behavior, there is no motivation to stay employed and deal with the potential unpleasant issues that can accompany responsibility.

Question #1: Are there areas of your young person's life (no matter the age) where you are allowing him or her to quit, give up, or not follow through on things he/she has started?

Abuse #2: Calling 911-- "Come fight this fire!"

The match: Like most mistakes, this one starts early and grows like the flame from a single match that grows into a forest fire. It starts early in life when two siblings have a conflict. One runs to Mom or Dad for justice. Judgment is passed on the apparent offender. Over time, the children learn that Mom or Dad or some other authority figure will always be there to solve their every conflict with others. As a result, they never learn to solve problems on their own.

The camp fire: The small flame that started at home now grows a little larger outside the home. The parent (usually the dad) is sitting in the first row watching his young son's ball game. The moment he thinks his son is not getting enough playing time, isn't being played in the proper position, has been improperly shifted in the batting order, or the referee has made a bad call, Dad is on the coach's or referee's case. Of course this is the same dad who was nowhere to be seen when there was a call for volunteer coaches. But he is quick to correct all the perceived wrongdoing and the first to defend his boy. The son, however, quickly learns that Dad is there to step in and solve all his problems for him.

The bonfire: The problem grows even bigger during the teenage years. A young man shows some promise in track and field in high school, but has some conflicts with the coach. He complains to his dad that he is not getting fair treatment on the team. Since Dad is on the school board and has some perceived authority to wield, he decides to set the coach straight, and he does. Dad, once again saves the day by coming to the rescue, and the boy learns once again that someone will always be there to solve the problem. Since the young man has never had to solve very many problems on his own, he slowly becomes a "cripple," never having the experience of working through his own challenges.

The forest fire: After years of unconscious conditioning that someone will always be there to fight his battles, the young person's problem starts raging out of control.   The older teenage young man is out late one night with friends who vandalize a local building. Word of mouth points back to the boy who is then confronted. In order to keep the incident from becoming a legal matter, the parents step in and offer to pay for the damage to be repaired.   The boy loses a few privileges, but is otherwise let off the hook.   Once again being rescued, the boy is freed from legitimate accountability.   His brush with the law has been averted this time.   But not really having learned a lesson, this fire is likely to burn out of control until the next time when the offense is too large for him to be saved and he is forced to stand on his own to deal with the consequences.

Question #2: Are you guilty of rescuing your young people by solving problems or resolving conflicts for them that they could learn from by solving for themselves?

Abuse #3: Calling 911–"It hurts. Get me out of pain!"

Part of growing up is learning the natural law of cause and effect-- that for every action there is an equal and opposite reaction. Sometimes learning that lesson can be emotionally painful.   In an effort to save the child from any suffering, parents come to the rescue in different ways to prevent the pain, but by so doing prevent any lesson from being learned.

There's always next time! Little Savana knows that if she doesn't clean up her room before school, she can't go out to play with her friends after school. The rule has been reviewed over and over until there is no doubt that she understands. But one morning she spends a little too much time doing this and that, and then rushes off to school without giving her room much thought.

Coming home from school that afternoon, she has grand plans to go over to a friend's house to play. She is confronted with, "But you didn't clean your room and you know what the rule is." She's remorseful now and runs to tidy up the room a bit. After returning from her now cleaned-up room she pleads incessantly, "Please let me go. All of my friends are going to be there. I'm going to be the only one who's not there. I promise I'll do it next time." Finally, to promote some peace and quiet, the parent in question chooses mercy over justice by saying, "OK. I'll let you go if you promise to do it next time." And off she goes, having learned once again that rules are easily broken, and that actions have consequences but only after you break the rules so many times you can't talk your way out of them.

Money talks! In an effort to teach the value of a dollar, Andrew's parents have set up an allowance system for their early teenage boy. Andrew knows that he is responsible for the proper management of that money for certain expenses he has, including activities he wants to do with his friends. But somehow Andrew always finds month left over at the end of his money!

One Saturday all his friends decide to go and play paint ball--a game he loves. However he soon discovers he's spent all of his money on other things. In an emotional panic, he runs to the source of emergency financial funding and pleads his case, "I'll pay you back out of my next allowance. You can just take it out of what I get next month."

> Then out comes the wallet and the money, too,
> and off goes Andrew who's so happy with you!
> "Thanks Mom and Dad. You are the best!
> Next month I'll be sure to manage the rest."

He's happy for now. And so are you because he's off having fun and you can go peacefully about your business. But the price of this lesson will be much greater than the money given today. In most cases there will be many tomorrows, and the price will be higher and higher until the money quits talking and you start teaching.

Truth or consequences? A group of high school boys got together and skipped one of their classes. The act was fairly transparent to the teacher who confronted them by saying that unless they brought a note from home with a legitimate excuse for their absence, it would count against their grade.

The students pled with their parents, promising they would never do it again if they would just "come to the rescue" this one time. Notes were written. The absences were excused. And the boys learned the lesson that if you can bend the truth, you can avoid the consequence. Mom and Dad saved the day once again!

Breeding "catfish." A very successful business owner whose children were in their 20's and early 30's had apparently rescued or excused his children too many times. Half of them had either dropped out of school or were on the ten-year college plan, having shifted majors two or three times. The others couldn't keep jobs or provide for themselves. This father who was very successful in his own business, had raised an entire family of "catfish" who were aimlessly wandering through life, bumping into stuff with no clear direction and no need to find one since Dad kept coming to the rescue each and every time by solving their immediate problems with his money. Fortunately this Dad will have a big estate to pass on to his kids. They'll need it!

Question #3: In what ways do you rescue your young people by not following through on agreed upon discipline or not allowing them to experience the true consequences of their actions?

From these examples, and others you may be able to perceive, it is obvious that with every level of development there is a corresponding level of responsibility to be addressed. The temptation to step in and rescue your children begins when they are very young. And the older they get, the more complex and entangled the problems become. It is tempting to provide emergency assistance to avoid temporary emotional discomfort when what is really needed is wisdom and a firm and caring hand.

"911 Emergency Rescue" Questions in Review

1. Are there any areas of your young person's life (no matter the age) wherein you are allowing him or her to quit, give up, or not follow through on things he/she has started?

2. Are you guilty of rescuing your young people by solving problems or resolving conflicts for them that they could learn from by solving themselves?

3. In what ways do you rescue your young people by not following through on agreed upon discipline, or not allowing them to experience the true consequences of their actions?

SOLUTION
Teach "First Aid" before You Go to the Rescue

Some lessons in life just have to be learned by experience. Deny the experience and you delay learning. Accept the experience and it can become a powerful teacher. Many Eagle "U" students have said that some of the greatest gifts they have been given have been at the hands of their parents who have:

- required follow through on commitments;
- allowed them to fight their own battles;
- given them the opportunity to face the consequences of their decisions.

While unpleasant at the moment, most of these young people later realized that the greatest gift their parents had given them was allowing them to do for themselves--letting them use their own "first aid" skills instead of always stepping in, coming to the rescue, and solving their problems for them.

Here are some of the valuable "first aid" lessons they have learned and how they learned them.

"First Aid" Skill #1
Commitment

Choose first and then follow through. Eagle "U" students who have learned the value of persistence, determination and follow through can most often point back to some experience they had early in life where a decision was initially made with a lot of help from Mom and Dad, and then the system was set up for the young person to follow through.

The system. The daughter of a very successful C.E.O. and a stay-at-home mom shared how she and all of her siblings were enrolled in music lessons by age eight. The children helped choose the instrument they would play. Some played the piano, others the violin or the trumpet. At the outset, the children clearly understood that they would take lessons for at least six years and then they could decide for themselves if they wanted to continue. When things got difficult and discouragement set in, quitting was never an option. They learned the lessons of persistence and determination. These parents set up the system to succeed from the beginning.

The set-up. With college tuition continuing to rise, the prospect of spending a year or two extra in school due to changing majors is an expensive proposition. Many Eagle "U" students we work with, who are on track to finish their college education in four years or less, have a college plan that was set up clearly from the outset. Their parents, who are providing financial assistance for college, have made it clear that the financial aid will be available as long as a certain grade point average is maintained and for four years, no longer.

When the rules are set up from the beginning, daily decisions are a lot easier to make along the way. Eagle "U" students on this system tell us that they think twice before procrastinating their study time, and rarely change their major which would further delay graduation.

The early warning! This lesson was learned at the hands of very wise parents--my own! I'm sure raising seven children was no easy task. There were many things that were made very clear to all of us early on in a very loving way. In our teenage years we were taught and re-taught, warned and forewarned, that when the time came that we decided to get married, along with that decision came the personal financial responsibility to support ourselves. The message was, **"If you are old enough to get married, you are old enough to take care of yourself."**

Those expectations being clear from the outset helped guide our emotional and romantic desires along the way!

"First aid" quiz question: What can you do to better set up the system in your children's lives so they make better decisions early and then follow through on their commitments?

"First Aid" Skill #2
Allowing your children to fight their own fires

Learning the skills to resolve your own conflicts is one of the most needed skills in our society today. From the very first session of Eagle "U," we have quoted the following people-skills facts:

• In most any career field, 15% of success is due to technical ability and skill on the job, while 85% of success is due to the ability and willingness to be dependable and to successfully deal with people.

• For every person who loses his or her job because of failure to perform the work properly, there are two people who lose their jobs because they cannot get along well with others.

Helping your young people to learn how to fight their own fires--to resolve the conflicts that may come their way--can be one of the most valuable skills they learn early in life to help them avoid the "catfish catastrophe."

Starting the training early. One of the most destructive people problems in any work place is gossip and the infant form of gossip, tattling. The dynamic is exactly the same in both cases--run to someone and tell all in order to avoid dealing with the issues yourself. In the training we do with professionals and business people, we establish a rule in the organization which is that everyone agrees to take all problems back to the source. If someone has a problem with another person in the workplace, it is his/her job to take the initiative to sit down with that person and sort out their differences. Many people struggle with the skills to do that.

Imagine the difference later in life if all children were required to resolve their own conflicts with siblings and friends with some coaching from an adult when needed. Those skills learned early in life would pay off well in adulthood. Teaching the skills of sitting down, listening, understanding where the other person is coming from, and determining a solution that both can live with takes time, patience, and the willingness to go through the process on a spur of the moment basis. It is never convenient. But the most important teaching moments seldom are.

"First aid" quiz question: When was the last time you got "sucked into" resolving a conflict between your young people when one of them came running to you for justice? How would you handle it differently today in order to teach them how to better resolve their own conflicts? How will you handle similar situations in the future?

Fighting fires at school: An English teacher at one of our local high schools gave a required reading assignment of a book that many considered to be of a questionable moral nature. While most parents were talking with each other and preparing to confront the teacher, one enlightened parent beat them all to the punch. Father and son sat down and discussed the nature of the book and mutually agreed that it was not in keeping with the values that they espoused as a family. With coaching from Dad, the son went to the teacher with his objection to the book and with a proposed solution. He said, "Based on the way I was brought up, my parents would not allow me to read this book if I had selected it myself. It just isn't the kind of thing we believe in. So would you give me permission to substitute another book that would be mutually acceptable in order to complete this assignment?"

The teacher was so impressed with this student's courage to stand up for what he believed that she went along with it willingly. The boy learned a valuable lesson and gained a whole new set of people skills in resolving differences with authority figures.

What if the teacher had not gone along with the proposal? Then, and only then, would the parents in this case have stepped in to fulfill their parental responsibility. This would be only after giving their son the opportunity to stand up for himself and to learn the lessons early that he will so desperately need later in life.

"First aid" quiz question: What opportunities have come up recently where you were tempted to step in and resolve a conflict with an authority figure for your young person that he/she could have had the opportunity to resolve? How will you handle similar situations in the future?

"First Aid" Skill #3:
Choose your cause because the effect will choose you!

Stepping in to save a young person from the consequences of a poor decision can be one of the most damaging "gifts of kindness" a parent can give. Learning to live with the consequences of our own decisions can be one of the more painful, but more valuable lessons we learn in life, for both parent and young person. Without those lessons learned by experience, the risk of the young person becoming an emotional and social cripple is increased. **Just remember that when you spare the consequence, you cripple the child.**

Occasionally, though rarely, we have young people come to Eagle "U" under duress. Mom and Dad tell them they have to come "or else." Typically such students are required to demonstrate a desire to attend on their own before they are granted admission.

Such was the case of a young woman who had recently graduated from high school. She wanted to attend Eagle "U"-- kind of! During the later part of her senior year, she participated in a covert senior slough day. Most of the students got away with it one way or another, but this unfortunate young lady got caught in the act. Because of similar previous infractions at home and at school, her parents made her "pay the price." Part of that price, among other things, was attendance at Eagle "U."

When she arrived, she was still upset with her parents. "The injustice of it all," she said. "It just wasn't fair, especially since all of my friends got away with it."

As the week progressed and lessons of success were learned, her perspective changed and she realized the potential path she had been on. She also recognized the wisdom of her parents in setting her straight early, and letting her experience the consequences of her action instead of "coming to the rescue."

By the last day of the course she said, "The hardest thing I will have to do now is return home and thank my parents for giving me this experience, and for allowing me to learn important lessons from experience instead of saving me from my own mistakes."

Fortunately, this young woman got the message early and was able to see the wisdom in her parents' ways. For others who are not quite so lucky, it may take longer--years longer. A very wise man thousands of years ago said: "Train up a child in the way he should go: and when he is old, he will not depart from it" (Proverbs 22:6). It seemed to be true then. It seems to be true today!

"First aid" quiz question: When was the last time you stepped in to save your young people from the consequences of their own decisions? Did they really learn the lesson they needed to learn from that situation? How will you respond differently next time in a similar situation?

An emotionally painful lesson for the parent. One of my mentors was the late Bill Gove, the first president of the National Speakers' Association. In one of his signature stories, Bill told of a phone call he received late one night from a friend who had discovered that Bill's son, Bill Jr., had just been arrested for having an open container of beer in his car while driving. This was strictly prohibited in the state of Minnesota where they lived.

"If we act quickly, I can keep this out of the papers and no one will ever find out," offered Bill's attorney friend.

"If you do, I'll have you disbarred!" exclaimed Bill. "The boy knows better. Let them print it in the paper. I want everyone to know. It will teach the boy a lesson." And so the attorney left the case alone.

Sure enough, the story ended up in the local newspaper. The only problem was that the editors of the paper left the "Jr." off the boy's name in the story!

Sometimes the consequences of "Jr.'s" actions are just as painful for Mom and Dad as they are for the young person! The lesson, however, still needs to be learned. So you choose. Let them experience the consequences of their actions today while the stakes are lower, or wait until the stakes are so high it may negatively effect the rest of their lives and yours!

"First aid" quiz question: What will you do in the future if confronted with a potentially painful consequence for you or your young person that might be more conveniently averted by your coming to the rescue? When will the lesson be learned?

"First Aid" Summary Quiz

1.   What can you do to better set up the system in your young people's lives so they make better decisions early and then follow through on their commitments?

2.   When was the last time you got "sucked into" resolving a conflict between your young people when one of them came running to you for justice? How would you handle it differently today in order to teach them how to better resolve their own conflicts? How will you handle similar situations in the future?

3. What opportunities have come up recently where you were tempted to step in and resolve a conflict with an authority figure for your young person that he/she could and should have had the opportunity to resolve? How will you handle similar situations in the future?

4. When was the last time you stepped in to save your young people from the consequences of their own decisions? Did they really learn the lesson they needed to learn from that situation? How will you respond differently next time in a similar situation?

5. What will you do in the future if confronted with a potentially painful consequence for you or your young person that might be more conveniently averted by your coming to the rescue? When will the lesson be learned?

MISTAKE 10
Following the "Do As I Say, Not As I Do" Philosophy

If you want to see what is really going on in a young child's mind, just observe and listen to a playtime session of "pretend."

"I'll be the mommy and you be the daddy."

What happens next is usually a direct reflection of what children observe going on at home and elsewhere in their world.

That world of pretend is just a dress rehearsal for future reality. Children audition for their parts based on the scripts and actors they have seen and observed. And the actor they observe the most is you!

Fortunately or unfortunately, depending on the role model, we all learned our parts early in life more by observation than we did by verbal instruction.

Learning first by example. In my own experience, one of the first great proofs of this principle came when my own words started coming out of the mouths of our young children. Sometime back, I had developed the habit of saying "Oh, man" every time something unfortunate or unexpected happened. The expression came to my attention one night when I told our youngest child it was time to get ready for bed. Barely in her first year of being able to express herself verbally she exclaimed, "Oh, man!" The rest of the family erupted into laughter at hearing Dad's echo.

Just do what I say! What comes most naturally is learning by example. What comes with the most difficulty is learning by command. One of the weakest commands in parental language comes after the inquiry from a young person who asks why he or she has to do something. "Because I said so," comes the parental reply.

More often than not, the only reason the "why" question comes up is because the young person has never seen the principle taught by example.

Examine these "Do as I say, not as I do" examples to see if any of the following (or similar ones) are present in your life:

☐ Mom pleads with all the family members to keep their rooms clean and make their beds while the master bed is rarely made.

☐ Dad always gives lectures on honesty, but when the phone rings and it is a salesman, he instructs the children, "Tell him I'm not home."

☐ Siblings are admonished to be nice to each other, while Mom and Dad can frequently be heard arguing loudly with each other.

☐ Teenagers are given a time limit on their phone calls to friends, while Mom routinely carries on lengthy conversations with friends and neighbors.

☐ Parents become frustrated when a child is not ready on time for a family activity, while Mom or Dad are frequently late for outside commitments.

☐ High school age young people are chastised for skipping class, while just a few months before Dad called in to work sick so he could go and play golf.

☐ Children are instructed to respect authority and obey the law, while Dad has a "fuzz buster" in his car.

☐ Teenagers are counseled against using drugs because it is illegal and harmful, while Mom and Dad allow supervised drinking parties for their underage teenage children and their friends because "they are going to do it anyway."

□ Getting good grades and a college education is emphasized while Mom or Dad never finished college themselves.

Young People of All Ages Pay More Attention to What You Do than to What You Say

One of our guest faculty members at Eagle "U" is a former professional football player who is now a father of several teenagers. He openly illustrates this principle to parents and students alike.

His daughter, who was in high school, was caught helping a friend cheat on a homework assignment. The friend had a lot going on and hadn't had time to finish an assignment for a class the two had together. Since the assignment was due the next day, the friend asked the daughter if she could borrow and copy her assignment with the promise that it would be returned to her in the hall before the class started.

But the following day, the two girls missed each other in the hallway and the daughter proceeded to class so she wouldn't be late. The friend rushed in at the last minute and handed the paper back to the daughter. The teacher easily perceived what was going on. She accused both girls of cheating because she felt that the person who allows someone else to copy is just as guilty as the one who does the copying.

After the phone call came to the home, the father proceeded to give his daughter the prescribed and much repeated lecture about honesty. While doing so he had a flashback. It was about the visits the family regularly made to a local fast food restaurant. He recalled that on these occasions, he would buy everyone a dinner, but instead of buying soft drinks for each one, he would buy only two because the restaurant had unlimited refills. That way all family members could drink as much as they wanted at a fraction of the cost.

As there was a pause in the father's lecture, the daughter provided her only defense which was "Everybody does it." That's exactly the excuse the father had given for his drink scheme. The daughter was obviously learning more from the father's behavior than she was from his lectures.

Perhaps the true power of this principle is why ancient prophets instructed and warned that the sins of the fathers would be passed on to their children for three to four generations. We just keep on doing what we have seen the most powerful influences in our life do. And so, your example, good or bad, will always have more teaching power than any other form of education or discipline.

The "Do As I Say" Self-exam

1. What are some things I see my young person doing that I may have been guilty of doing myself?

2. In what areas do I find my children asking why they have to do something when they may not have seen by example what I am asking them to do?

3. What are the most powerful lessons I have taught or am teaching the young people in my life by my example - good or bad?

4. Is there anything I ask of the young people in my life that I am not willing to do, or have not done myself?

SOLUTION
"Do As I Do"

If you have been around an infant recently, you've been reminded of the first and most fundamental way we initially learn everything - by imitation. Just watch a mother with a young infant:

* When she smiles, the infant smiles back.
* When she moves her head back and forth, the infant tries to do the same.
* When she makes a sound, the infant tries to imitate.

Our very first words are learned by imitation as well. My two older "Yankee" sisters learned to read in an elementary school in Roanoke, Virginia, at the hand of a good woman who spoke with a very traditional southern accent. The power of her example and their unintentional imitation of her accent were very evident. In ordinary conversation, my sisters spoke with their normal western United States accent which they learned when they learned to talk while living in the West. But when they opened a book and read out loud, they sounded downright Southern! Since their teacher had taught them how to convert the written word into sounds, they copied her exact pronunciation. It didn't occur to them at their young age that there is a relationship between reading out loud and speaking.

We Are More than Half of What We Are by Imitation

If we learn the most powerful lessons by imitation, what are your children learning from your example? What beliefs, attitudes and behaviors are they learning directly from your actions?

What were the most powerful lessons you learned from your own parents, mentors, and teachers? If you are like most, your mind immediately goes back to experiences you had with those people who taught you an unforgettable lesson. Meanwhile, we seldom remember lectures, advice or verbal counsel unless it is later confirmed by example.

Action has ten times the teaching impact of verbal instruction. The eyes and ears are active all the time.

There are three primary areas where all of us learn by example. Consider what the young people in your life are learning from you in these three areas:

1. What you do speaks louder than what you say.
2. How you treat your young people will determine how they treat others later on.
3. How your young person observes you treating the older children in the family signals how he/she can anticipate being treated.

Here are some observations in of each of these areas:

1. *What you do speaks louder than what you say.*

The Parable of the Shoes

T'was a terrible problem with the shoes you'll learn,
Scattered and left at every turn.
When you walked in the door
To the stairs and the landing,
A pair of shoes could be found
Where you were standing.

The mom of the house,
She would beg and would plead
With everyone, "Pick up your shoes, if you please.
It's quite a great mess,
Putting me to the test
To keep the house clean.
It's rare to be seen."
But day after day and night after night,
The mom of the house put the shoes out of sight.

The problem persisted, grew worse by the day
Until she discovered a much better way.
The problem, it ended the way it began
With a small simple gesture begun by a man.
As soon as the dad took his boots by himself
From the family room floor to his closet shelf,
The kids got the message, one that's not hollow.
His action was all that they needed to follow.

So what is the moral? The word or the deed?
The *deed* of course has the power to lead.

Actions speak louder than words. What leaders say has a greater impact on their followers than just what they say. Military history, for example, is replete with incidents that turned the tide of a battle because a commander - an infantry platoon leader or a general - put himself in harm's way while shouting the command, "Follow me." It does not seem strange, then, that "Follow me" is the slogan of the

Infantry branch of the United States Army. It is a direction that could well be a standard for every parent, the most important and influential leader a young person will ever have.

2. *How you treat your young people will determine how they will treat others later on.* We seldom forget how we are treated, especially in potentially emotional situations. How we are treated as young people in those situations usually sets a pattern for our treatment of others when it is our turn to dominate.

It all comes from the fact that the lessons that last the longest are cemented in our hearts and minds with some type of emotional experience. The emotion anchors the lesson for a lifetime.

Several years ago, one of my brothers was teaching his oldest daughter to drive. Since she had recently received her driver's license, they were working on the finer points of driving safety. One day they were returning home and she was pulling the car into the garage, being careful to clear the wall on the left and the other car parked on the right. At the final moment she accidentally hit the gas pedal instead of the brake, and ran the car straight into the back wall of the garage.

Now what is a father to do in this situation? What should he say? What could he say?

Before a word slipped out of his mouth, an image immediately popped into his mind. It was from many years earlier when he had done something very similar as a teenager and our most thoughtful father only responded to him with love, understanding and a greater concern for the driver than for the damaged car and garage.

In turn, my brother did the same - passing the gift of his own father on to his daughter. It was an experience neither father nor daughter will ever forget.

How you treat your young people will more often than not become the way they will treat others around them and ultimately how they will treat their own children.

3. *How your young person observes you treating the older children in the family signals how he/she can anticipate being treated.* Childhood memories are filled with powerful images. Some are good and some are bad. At some age we are able to distinguish between the way we are treated and the way others are treated around us. But to some extent, how others are treated by our role models sends a very powerful message about how we will likely be treated.

At Eagle "U" we start working with teenagers at age fourteen. Most of these young people talk about their older siblings and how they are treated by their parents. They know it is a sign of things to come for themselves.

Kyle was in his early teens when I met him for the first time at Eagle "U." He had a sister who was about eight years older. She had a lot of psychological problems that went undiagnosed for many years. Because of her illness, she had created a lot of problems for the entire family. Kyle told me about the great patience and love his parents had shown his sister even when they received little or none of it back from her for many years. "My parents are pretty amazing people," he said. "I don't know how they do it."

I have followed the whole family situation as Kyle has returned to Eagle "U" through his high school and college years. Kyle's sister was finally diagnosed and received the proper medical attention she needed. Kyle has developed into one of the finest young men we have ever had at Eagle "U." His respect for his parents continues. And although he sacrificed as a child because of the chaos that his sister created in their home, the way his parents handled her sent him a clear message that has given him a strong feeling of security. If they would care for his sister like they did with all of her problems, he knew that they would always love and care for him as well.

Letting Your Young Person Take the Lead

At some point it is time to test the waters and see what impact your example is having in the lives of your young people. So let them take the lead on decisions and see how you (and they) are doing.

Shortly before Tom headed off to college, he and his father decided it would be a good idea to replace the car he was driving so he would have something more reliable for the next four years. They advertised the used car for several weeks in the newspaper, and after numerous showings they finally found a full price buyer. After all of the details had been worked out, the prospective buyer made one last request that was a condition of the purchase. He wanted a receipt from the seller establishing the sale price as $2,500 instead of the actual price of $5,000. This would not have any effect on the seller, but would reduce the amount of sales tax the buyer would be required to pay the state. The buyer agreed to come back later that day with a cashier's check to complete the transaction.

As the prospective buyer drove away, Tom's father turned to him and asked, "What do you think we should do?"

Together they decided they would risk losing the sale rather than make a false statement. They told the buyer when he returned that if he wanted the car, they would have to write the receipt for the actual sales price.

Tom's dad had led by example for years. Tom knew what was right because he had seen his father do right in dozens of other situations. Now, when Tom was called on to take the lead and make the decision, he knew what to do.

Once the foundation has been laid, give your young people the opportunity to take the lead. The sooner they experience making the right decisions in your presence, the more likely they will be to make the right ones when you're not around.

What If It Is Too Late?

Perhaps there are things you would like your young person to do that you may not have been a great example of in the past. You may be asking yourself if it is too late.

Perhaps it's not. Dave Thomas was the founder of Wendy's Hamburgers - one of the three leading fast food hamburger chains in the world. Dave never knew his birth mother and was adopted by a couple from Michigan at the age of six months. His adoptive mother died when he was five and by age ten he had lost two stepmothers. Life only got more complicated as he reached his teen years. He dropped out of high school when he was in the tenth grade in order to support himself.

His trail to success from that kind of start to having 6000 franchised outlets is a story in itself. With the business prospering and with others able to handle the day-to-day running of it, he took up two public service projects. One involved the encouraging of well functioning families to adopt children. The other was to encourage young people to stay with the education system and graduate from high school.

On one occasion he was encouraging a group of high school students to follow through to graduation. One of the students interrupted and asked why he had not followed his own advice and graduated himself. He realized that he was not a very worthy example or role model of what he advocated. So in the spirit of "do as I do," he picked up where he had left off so many years before and went back to the books. Eventually he passed the general education high school exam. He then donned a cap and gown and went through graduation exercises in 1993 at age 61, marching across the stage with a typical group of youthful students. He then felt he could continue moving about advocating high school graduation with the added power of his own example.

It's never too late to do the right thing.

Here Is the "Do As I Do" Formula

1. Give young people a good example to follow. They learn by imitation from day one.

2. Treat your young people the way you want them to treat others - including your future grandchildren!

3. Treat others right. Your young people will learn from your example and will anticipate being treated in the same manner.

4. Let them take the lead while you are still around. Once you have taught by example, let them make their own decisions while you still have a chance to guide and be at their side.

5. Start over if you need to and change your ways. Do it! Your example, no matter how late, can have a powerful and positive impact on your young person's life.

MISTAKE 11
Failing to Teach That Right Is Right and Wrong Is Wrong

It was a defining moment in American history and a sad day for those who know that a country is only as strong as its moral fiber. An American president sat for intense questioning in front of a grand jury. If there is one phrase that will go down in history as the most infamous phrase of his eight-year administration it is, "I did not have sex with that woman."

As he became the laughing stock of American politics, there were also many who wept. They were not tears of sympathy, but tears of sorrow, knowing that the man who held the most powerful position in the free world had sent a very clear, powerful, and false message to young and old alike: **right is right and wrong is right; it all depends on how you look at it.**

There is ample evidence to suggest that he was not alone in his belief. In the wake of his administration we've seen some of the largest corporate scandals in history where high-level corporate executives have exhibited their own definition of right by approving accounting procedures that were clearly wrong but gave them immediate financial reward in terms of high stock values and inflated earnings reports. I'm sure they figured out a way to justify this as being right. But they didn't get off as easily as their role model in the White House.

Somewhere in the past these men never learned that right is right and wrong is wrong. And so with power and prestige came the test: Would they go ahead and define their own right even when it was wrong, or do what is right because it was the right thing to do? It was a test that many of them failed. It destroyed their careers. It destroyed their reputations. More tragically, it did irreparable damage to thousands of innocent victims who were directly or indirectly affected by their poor judgment.

Where do young people learn right from wrong? The rising generation learns much of its moral lessons from one of the most powerful socializing forces in our culture - the media - which reports and interprets events in politics, business and life in general. Let's take a look at some of the "right is right and wrong is right" messages that are reinforced every day in the minds of our young people and often in the minds of adults who do not have sound moral convictions:

❏ **From politicians —**
Message: "I think most Americans are smart enough to separate the behavior in his (the president's) personal life from his political life."

Underlying Lesson: It doesn't matter what you do behind closed doors as long as you put on the right appearance in public.

❏ **From the courts —**
Message: "He was acquitted on a technicality."

Underlying Lesson: You can get away with it as long as you have some technical alibi that will get you off the hook.

❏ **From television —**
Message: "Everybody's doing it."

Underlying Lesson: That many people can't be wrong.

While young people are absorbing these examples from the media, what are the lessons they are learning at home? How you handle specific situations in their lives will teach them more about what is right and what is wrong than any lecture, lesson or speech you can give.

How would you handle these common "right is right and wrong is right" traps? They are actual case studies from the lives of young people. What would you do as a parent in these situations?

■ **Trap:** *"I didn't have a choice. They made me do it."*
A fraternity at the university your young person is attending brings a keg of beer to the fraternity house and the members have a party. The pledges, most of whom are under legal drinking age, are pressured into the party to show they are not prudes and would fit into the fraternity culture. The party gets noisy and the neighbors call the police. A police raid results in the arrest of the underage drinkers along with those who brought the keg into the house. Your young person is among the underage who are arrested. The plea of the underage drinkers to their parents is that they really didn't have much choice. "They made me do it."

What would you do?

What would you say?

What can you do today to prevent this from happening to your young person?

■ **Trap:** *"No one else has to, so why should I?"*
You have set a curfew of 12:00 midnight for your high school age young person. Your young person stays out until 1:00 a.m. When accountability time arrives, the argument is that none of his friends involved have a curfew and no one would provide a ride home. "No one else has a curfew, so why should I?"

What would you say?

What would you do?

What can you do to prevent this from happening?

■ **Trap:** *"Everybody does it."*

Your high school senior participates in senior slough day without your knowledge. She and all of her friends skip class. You are the only parent of the young people in the group who is at home when the school officials call about the absence, so you are the only parent who knows about the unauthorized behavior. All the other kids write their own excuse notes and sign their parents' names so they will be admitted back in the class the next day. Your young person pleads with you, "Let's not make a big thing of this. Just write me an excuse and it will all be over."

What would you say?

What would you do?

What can you do to prevent this from happening?

■ **Trap:** *Shifting the blame.*

A college student goes to a community near the university late one night and manages to hot-wire a very expensive luxury car that was on display at an auto dealership. He brings it back to school and suggests to three of his dorm buddies that they leave school at noon on Friday and take a joyride to a distant city and have a good time for the weekend. The plan is for the one who stole the car to return it to the car lot late Sunday night, and all of them to be back in school Monday morning. The plan is foiled when they get in an accident and total the car.

There is trouble with the police about the registration papers, but by Monday morning no charges have been filed. It appears to be up to the car dealer to press the charges. By this time, the father of the student who stole the car is faced with a major dilemma. He is a prominent community leader, a successful businessman, and he has several other children all of whom stand to suffer from the act of their errant brother. Now the father has a wrenching decision to make. Saving his reputation would certainly be worth the tens of thousands of dollars that it would take to reimburse the dealer for the car, and it might keep his son out of jail.

The parents of the other boys are confronted with the "shifting the blame" trap. These three knew that the car was stolen but maintained that they were not involved in any wrongdoing because they didn't steal the car.

As the parent of any one of the boys involved, what would you say?

What would you do?

What can you do to prevent this from ever happening?

■ **Trap:** *"They can't prove it."*
Your high school age young person helps some other students cheat on an exam. All those involved have been confronted with the suspicion, but there is no hard evidence to prove what has happened. Your young person's friends are all saying, "They can't prove it."

What would you tell your young person?

What would you do?

What can you do to prevent this from happening?

■ **Trap:** *"It wasn't wrong - technically."*
Your junior high school age student has been fined ten dollars for incidental damage and loss of some classroom materials at school. She takes issue with the way the teacher handled the entire situation. Without saying a word to you, she returns to school and pays the fine by ceremoniously dumping a thousand loose pennies on the teacher's desk. You are called to the school after the furious teacher has sent your student to the principal's office for disciplinary action. Your student defends herself by saying, "I paid the fine didn't I? I didn't do anything wrong - technically."

What would you say?

What would you do?

What can you do today to prevent something like this from happening?

Do You Ever Fall for the "Wrong Is Right" Trap?

What is or would be your response to these "wrong is right" disguises?

* "I didn't have a choice. They made me do it."

* "No one else has to, so why should I?"

* "Everybody does it."

* Shifting the blame.

* "They can't prove it."

* "It wasn't wrong - 'technically'."

What other "wrong is right" traps have you seen that you can start preventing your young person from falling into today?

SOLUTION
Right Is Right Is <u>Right!</u>

The way you handle situations like those we have mentioned above leaves an imprint on your young people's minds. The influence that imprint has on future decisions and behavior may have a much greater impact on their lives than those that created the original dilemma.

If they can get away with it today, what kind of message does that send to them about what they might be able to get away with tomorrow? Besides, if Mom or Dad don't see anything wrong with it, how wrong could it really be?

Action: Decide today where you stand when it comes to situations like these and **begin reinforcing what is right.** The most powerful example will be the way you handle the definition of right and wrong in your own life and how you deal with it in relation to your young people. Another source of example can come from stories of people of distinction who have made right decisions. These will have lasting impact on young people as they make decisions on their own later.

One of my most cherished childhood memories is of the bedtime stories Dad often read to me about the lives of early inventors, heroes and other people of note whose decisions changed the world. From those stories I learned about Thomas Edison's persistence which produced the electric light, the record player, and hundreds of other useful inventions. I came to know George Washington and his honesty, virtue and honor. I heard about Eli Whitney and his ability to think differently than others which enabled him to invent the first cotton gin. Through the pages and pictures in the books Dad read to me I met and came to admire many others such as Robert Fulton who invented steam power to propel boats despite the ridicule and criticism of those who said it could not be done. All these people had values and virtues to be admired. Each of them made critical decisions that had dramatic outcomes. Their stories, so firmly planted in my young mind years ago, have remained with me and continue to be an influence. Their examples have had a powerful impact on my life as I have faced my own decisions. The lives of these great people have given me models to follow and their examples have been a foundation to build on. **Give your young people great examples to follow in the form of images of exemplary men and women they will never forget.**

When the Right Answer Isn't the Only Answer

What do you do when there isn't a moral, ethical or legal right or wrong? It may be your opinion against your young person's, or your desires against his or hers. What do you do? What do you say? How you react could determine a lesson learned.

Example: Johnny is a junior in high school who comes home from school one day and declares, "I'm dropping out of school. I hate school. It's worthless. The teachers all hate me. Besides, I'm bored. I could be learning so much more if I were just out in the real world working."

The typical parental response is usually, "Johnny, you can't drop out of school. You won't be able to get a job. Besides, how are you going to support yourself for the rest of your life? You obviously have not thought this through."

Now, what do you think Johnny's response will be? Do you really think he is going to say, "Oh, you're right. I haven't thought this out. I'm wrong again. Dumb me."

I don't think so. Since Johnny, like everyone else, doesn't want to be wrong, he will ignore the facts and set out to prove his position - to prove he is right.

No one wants to be wrong. One of the greatest human fears is that of being identified as saying or doing something wrong. None of us wants to be wrong, and so we will defend our right to be right!

Have you ever noticed that most young people, like their older peers, will defend their obviously wrong position just so they can seem to be right? How often do you put your young people in the position of defending their views just because they don't want to be wrong?

How to give the right response in order to get the right action. Imagine Johnny's reaction if the parental response to his "I'm quitting school" declaration were something like this:

Parent: "Hm, OK. Whatever you decide is OK. But before you make a final decision, how about if we take a look at the consequences and results of a far-reaching decision like this. Let's draw a line on this piece of paper. On the left side we'll write,

'Drop out of School.' On the right we'll put, 'Stay in School.'

"Now let's write the consequences of staying in school. --- It sounds like you think you will be bored. You'll have to put up with teachers you think don't like you. I'm sure there are some other unpleasant things you'll have to put up with. Am I right?

"So let's hop over to the other column for a moment. Tell me the benefits of dropping out of school. --- You won't have to put up with any more teachers. You'll be able to go out and earn your own money. You won't have to sit through boring classes, etc.

"Now let's go back to the 'Stay in School' column. Tell me what you think some of the positive effects of finishing your education might be. --- Better job opportunities, a higher income, more freedom to live where you want to, and a better lifestyle.

"Now let's write down the potential negative consequences of quitting school. --- Getting a job might be a lot more difficult. Higher paying jobs will be harder to come by. Future earning potential will probably be lower. You'll have less freedom to live where you want to live and go where you want to go, etc.

"Now, based on the results of those two directions, which list do you think will give you the best outcome in the long term?"

As you go through this discussion, make sure that it is just that - a discussion, not a lecture. Stay focused on results, not who is right and who is wrong. When Johnny has the freedom to choose a result without running the risk of being labeled as wrong, he is more likely to choose the right direction.

Will this always work? I don't know of any approach that works with 100% of the people 100% of the time. But when you take all of the judgment out of the exchange and become a partner in the process instead of a judge, the outcome is more likely to be in the right direction for your young person's future.

This approach can apply to moral things as well. For instance, high school age student, Don, is caught smoking. Most likely he is going to get a lecture containing phrases such as, "That's going to kill you. It's bad for you. Besides, you're too young."

What's Don going to do? He will most likely defend his position and keep on doing what he wants to do because he wants to feel that he is right.

A better solution might be to say, "So you're smoking. Tell me what you like about it." Your discussion might center around friends who are doing it; it's the "in" thing to do; he doesn't want to be left out, etc.

Then the conversation continues. "What are some of the risks you might be taking if you decide to continue to smoke?" --- Getting expelled from school; getting kicked off the team; not being able to attract the most desirable girls.

And then comes your final question. "Don, I think I know what you really want. I only want the best for you. How can I help you get it?"

If you are concerned that your teenager won't open up to you to even discuss the matter, just start by removing the judgment. No one wants to be judged because judges usually rule first on right and wrong. We don't want to be wrong, so we avoid the judge at all costs.

Our job is to educate. The greatest success gift a parent can give a child is a good education. The Latin base of this word is "educe" which means to bring out or develop from latent or existing information - to elicit. Education does not occur merely from providing information. It occurs when there is understanding and acceptance of the ideas presented. If you have laid the moral groundwork in the early years, then all you have to do is draw it out in the later years. It's there just waiting to come out and be developed.

Action Items for Teaching
That Right Is Right and Wrong Is Wrong

1. Decide today how you are going to handle the "wrong is right" traps.

2. Give your young people good examples to live up to. Read and study together the lives of exemplary people.

3. Quit being the judge and start being the educator. Don't accuse your young people of taking a wrong position so they feel the need to defend it. Focus on potential results and let them take the responsibility for drawing the right conclusions.

MISTAKE 12
Failing to Put Money in the Proper Perspective

Picture this. It is an uncharacteristically quiet moment at Eagle "U." All of the college age students are assembled and I am at the front of the group. I have just asked a question that has caused everyone to think: *"How many of you know how much money your parents make each year in order support the lifestyle your family has?"*

There are some glances around the room. After some hesitation, about 25% of the students raise their hands.

Then comes my next question: *"Why would it be important for you to know the answer to that question?"*

Again, there are more glances around the room. After some hesitation a discussion ensues in which we discuss the **Income Thermostat.**

What function does a thermostat have? It regulates the temperature of a room or a building. If the thermostat is set at 72 degrees and the temperature dips down to 70 or 71 degrees, it triggers the heating system to warm the room temperature back up to 72 degrees. If the room temperature gets too high, the thermostat triggers the air conditioning system to cool things down to 72 degrees.

Just as that thermostat is set to regulate room temperature, all of us have a subconscious income thermostat that is set to regulate the lifestyle at which we are most comfortable. That lifestyle becomes the standard which each person expects to maintain. More often than not, that standard is set and/or is greatly influenced by the lifestyle one experiences as a child and as a youth.

The positive part of having such an expectation is that the lifestyle is desirable and worth acquiring. The negative part is that one might fail to acquire an understanding of the time, effort, education, and insight that it takes to acquire and maintain that lifestyle.

As I discuss this matter with young people, I customarily ask them if it would be a good idea to consider the importance of maintaining a certain lifestyle as they choose their career and the pathway to it. This helps to emphasize that it is necessary to choose an occupation that has the potential to produce the income that will support the anticipated lifestyle. As we discuss this issue, there are usually several who are in need of a reality check. It might be well to consider how many of the following symptoms you have seen in your own young person or others in this age group:

The college "catfish." Of course we all know there are important factors other than income that need to be considered in choosing a career --things such as natural talents, likes and dislikes, nature of the work, etc. But more often than not, young people become figurative catfish in their college years as they change from one major to another. Initially they may have chosen a major based on what they liked to study, and then found that there are few occupations in that major that have the potential to provide their desired standard of living. So they change majors several times. This is one of the reasons the average college student today is so successful at cramming a four-year college curriculum into six years!

The confused coed. Occasionally we come across college age students who have given little or no thought to their earning potential in any given field. They may have the illusion that they will always have available to them all of the lifestyle benefits they have always had while growing up. After all, they reason, these things have always been there. Mom and Dad have always been there to pick up the slack. Why should anything change?

The marriage menagerie. At Eagle "U" I put both young men and young women on notice to make a mental note about the lifestyle in which their future spouse has been raised. More often than not, that is the lifestyle to which he/she has become accustomed and will feel most comfortable maintaining. If the primary breadwinner is more comfortable at a lower income level than the primary caregiver, real budget problems can plague the marriage. Conversely, if the primary caregiver is comfortable at a lower income level than the primary breadwinner, there may be very little patience on the part of the caregiver as to why so much time, effort and energy are expended making a living. A problem with money is one of the top two causes of divorce. Failure to work on the income thermostat in a marriage relationship is one of the biggest reasons people turn into "catfish" in their married life - running from one relationship to another because they have no clear marriage map.

Mistaken Certainties

Someone wisely said, "It ain't what you don't know that gets you in trouble, it's what you do know that ain't so." Over the years, some young people develop beliefs that aren't necessarily so, and it may take years of trial and error to correct them. Do you see any signs of the following mistaken certainties in your young people?

Mistaken Certainty #1: *Rights are free.*

Earlier in the chapter on The Entitlement Trap, we talked about the confusion between rights and privileges. Most young people view getting a driver's license as a right when they turn sixteen. Few have an understanding of the financial impact of having a young person licensed and allowed to drive a car. Many teens are not aware that the day they get a driver's license the automobile insurance rate on any car they are allowed to drive doubles or triples since teens are statistically in the very highest risk group. Increased maintenance, repairs and gas become part of the picture. Then there is the increased potential for physical harm and the liability for other drivers and pedestrians.

I routinely ask juniors and seniors in high school who attend Eagle "U" how many of them know how much auto insurance costs for a car that has a driver under age twenty-five. Less than 25% have any idea. If there is no understanding, there is no appreciation. So along with their illusion that driving is a right is their mistaken certainty that the right is free.

Mistaken Certainty #2: *What I want is what I need.*

During a late summer back-to-school shopping trip, Sue and Johnny reveal that they must have the most popular (and usually most expensive) name-brand shoes and clothes. Wearing what is "in" is viewed by them as a social necessity. All parents want their children to be socially well adjusted and fit in. And so, more often than not, they extend themselves financially to provide for their children's theoretical needs, while, by so doing, they are reinforcing the false perception that what their children want is what they must have.

Mistaken Certainty #3: *Immediate gratification has no price.*

While Sue and Johnny are looking on, the purchase for their "needed" school clothes is paid on Mom's or Dad's credit card. With a quick swipe of the card and a signature, the entire transaction is over and done with. Rarely is there ever a discussion about the interest charges that come along with that purchase if it is not paid off within thirty days. Perhaps this is the biggest reason college students are one of the largest target markets for credit card companies. Within days of turning legal age, the average college age student will receive multiple credit card offers. And he or she will likely graduate from college with thousands of dollars in credit card debt. Credit card companies are indebted to parents everywhere for reinforcing the false concept that immediate gratification is free!

Mistaken Certainty #4: *The significance of money is only in what it can buy without an understanding of what it takes to earn it.*

One of our Eagle "U" students graphically demonstrated this mistaken certainty. For the better part of the two-hour flight from her home town to the city where the Eagle "U" session was being held, she talked on the air phone that was conveniently in front of her. She was very aware that the cost of those calls was $2.50 a minute and that the total bill would be upwards of $300. She knew all of that. But since she had a healthy dose of "entitlement" she knew that Dad would cover it. "It's just $300" was her reply to her parents. All she knew was how much money would buy. But never having had to put in her own time to earn a dollar, she had no idea what it was really worth. What a dollar can buy is only a small part of the equation. What it takes to earn it is what determines its true value to the individual.

Mistaken Certainty #5: *Money makes you happy.*

When I ask young people to tell me what they want from a future career, the number one item on the list is always "a lot of money."

My next question is "How much is 'a lot'?" Very few can give a quantifiable answer. The mistaken certainty is that as long as there is enough money to go around, everything will be great.

The young people at Eagle "U" soon discover, through an extensive money management exercise, that more income usually means more bills, more responsibility, more headaches, and more work to maintain the higher standard of living. They soon discover that the secret is not necessarily more money, but knowing how to astutely manage the money they have.

Mistaken Certainty #6: *I can only earn what I earn with my own time and my own hands.*

Coming out of college, an acquaintance of mine monitored closely my job search. Having graduated from college just a few years before I did, I'm sure he was interested to see who, between the two of us, ended up landing the best paying job. Every time I received a job offer he asked, "How much are they going to pay you?" It became an obsession with him. When I eventually ended up taking a new company start-up opportunity that paid nothing - no salary, no guarantees of anything - he was dumbfounded. "Why would you do that?" he asked. He, like most other young people, had the mistaken certainty that the only value he could get from a job was what he could get paid immediately for his time invested.

Few young people, or adults for that matter, understand that there are two types of occupations: 1. Fee for service. 2. Fee for results. A mechanic, a dentist, a surgeon or a C.P.A. all get paid for performing a service for someone. More often than not, they are paid for their time and expertise. A business owner, manufacturer or investor gets paid for producing or getting an end result. There is a big difference between the two.

Freedom to go wherever you want to go whenever you want to go there doesn't come about just because you earn a lot of money. If you choose a labor intensive profession, it will require you to be on the job all of the time or the income ceases. The biggest career guidance mistake most parents make is the failure to teach lessons about leverage and career freedom instead of just focusing on finding a job or a career that makes a good income.

A Few Questions To Ask Yourself

How many of these mistaken certainties do your young people exhibit?

❏ What privileges have been confused as free rights in your young person's life for which there is no current price being paid?

❏ What areas in your young person's life does he/she perceive a want as a necessity?

❏ How recently was your young person given whatever he or she wanted with no discussion or realization of what the real cost was (immediate gratification)?

❏ How does your young person value money - in terms of what it can buy, or in terms of what it takes to earn it?

❏ Does your young person want a lot of money without having an understanding of the importance of managing that money?

❏ Does your young person understand the difference between getting paid a fee for hourly service and getting paid for an agreed upon end result (leverage)?

SOLUTION
Put Money in the Proper Perspective

There are specific steps you can take to reset the income thermostat in your young people and prevent the mistaken certainties about money from creating indecisive catfish behavior in:

* Buying decisions.
* College selection.
* Deciding on a college major.
* Getting married or remarried.
* Career selection.
* Many other decisions in life where money is involved.

Money Matter #1: *See that privileges are earned.*

Every child, every young person should have the right to a physically and emotionally safe home, healthy food, and a good education. Beyond these necessities most everything else is a privilege. And privileges should be earned.

In the real world, Bob doesn't get a vacation from his job until he has earned it by working a certain number of weeks or months, or by getting a certain result. Doesn't it follow then that little Bobby should learn this principle by finishing his homework, doing his chores etc. to earn free time?

Later, Bobby can earn time with his teenage friends by showing that he is responsible in following rules that have been set for behavior at home. He can earn future time with friends away from home by following rules that have been set for being home on time, reporting in periodically, etc.

In addition, Bobby can earn the right to get a driver's license by demonstrating responsible behavior. He can earn the right to drive the family car by participating in the additional cost for him to drive it. This can be by paying for a portion of the insurance cost, maintenance, or at least the cost of the gas he uses. The sooner Bobby understands about the total cost of driving the car, the better equipped he will be to face the real world and make smart decisions that are based on reality, not fiction.

Action: Think of other ways to help your young person understand and experience the reality that most things in life are privileges and privileges must be earned.

Money Matter #2: *Distinguish clearly between needs and wants.*

Nearly every parent struggles with a young person who wants to fit in. One of the perceived ways to accomplish this is by wearing the right clothes. The price of this kind of fitting in is not usually cheap.

Being the last of seven children, I have been the benefactor of the great examples of six older brothers and sisters who have done a great job of raising their children.

My oldest sister, Julie, came up with an ingenious idea that helped her four children learn the difference between needs and wants during their teenage years. Each year she would sit down with her children, one at a time, and talk about the family budget. She would go over the exact amount that had been set aside to cover their clothing needs for the year. After carefully explaining to them that their clothing budget was to cover all of their clothing needs for the year, she turned over each child's personal clothing budget to him or her to manage. If they chose more expensive brand names in shoes or anticipated the need for a prom dress, they learned that they were going to have to sacrifice in some other areas. If for any reason they could not buy everything they wanted and stay within the budget, they quickly learned that they would either have to go without or find a way to earn additional money to acquire their wants.

I've watched this system with great interest over the years and have been impressed with how all four children have learned to manage their emotions, and their money, and to clearly distinguish between needs and wants.

Interestingly enough, the same system has been followed through each child's college years. Education has always been viewed as a necessity in this home, and the parents were financially able and willing to pay for college tuition and books for each child. However, the costs of recreation, entertainment, transportation, etc. have always been the responsibility of each child. They have all had to find ways to provide for their own wants, and they have learned how to do it very well.

Action: Help the young people in your life to clearly distinguish between needs and wants, and give them an opportunity to earn the wants.

Money Matter #3: *Teach that ownership has its privileges.*

You'll remember that well-known phrase made popular by a certain credit card company - *Membership has its privileges.* Membership does have its "privileges" - one of which is the privilege of buying and owning more "stuff." And that stuff comes with a price.

Remember the question I posed to Eagle "U" students that opened this chapter? It was, "How many of you know how much money your parents make each year in order support the lifestyle your family has?"

While most haven't a clue, every once in a while there is a young person who surprises me.

Such was the case with Michael, the fifteen year-old son of a entrepreneur who lived in the mid-western part of the United States. Not only did Michael have a pretty good handle on the family income, he was very familiar with the family budget. His very astute parents started including him in money discussions in his early teenage years. He was plugged into the monthly grocery budget - mostly because he made up the majority of the expense, being a fast-growing teenage boy! He knew what the utilities cost each month. He was even allowed to look at the credit card bills from time to time and to see what the cost of credit card interest was if the balance was not paid off each month. He even knew how much the mortgage payment on the house was, including how much of that payment went toward principal and how much went toward interest!

I haven't met very many "Michaels" over the years of working with young people. I'm not sure it is necessary for a 15 year-old to be as familiar with the family finances as he was, but there was no question that Michael understood the price of immediate gratification as well as the price of ownership. There was also no question in my mind that when Michael went to college and received his first credit card application, he would know exactly what it meant and exactly what to do with it. Because of the great financial education he received at home, his risk of being caught in the credit trap later in life was dramatically reduced.

Action: Think of ways you can teach the principle that immediate gratification comes with a price and that "ownership has its privileges."

Money Matter #4: *Teach that the real value of money comes from the effort to earn it, not the cost to buy.*

The following script may sound vaguely familiar. The punch line, however, has been modified slightly from what you may have heard in the past!

New shoes for the prom: one hundred and twenty-five dollars. New evening gown: one hundred thirty-five dollars. Visit to the hair salon the day of the dance to look her best for the boy of her dreams: fifty dollars. The lesson Suzie learned about the real value of money by having to work over sixty plus hours at $7.50 an hour to earn enough money in order to purchase it all - PRICELESS!!!

Far too often young people are very familiar with the cost of everything they want, but it is not until they have the experience of having to put in the hours to earn the money to purchase those things that they make the long trip from illusion to reality. What something costs has very little to do with its true value to the individual. Understanding how many hours and how much effort it will take to make the money in order to cover the cost of what they want is what determines the real value.

Fast forward. Imagine twenty years later. Suzie is sitting with the boy of her dreams who is now her husband. They are discussing their budget, financial goals, and retirement costs with a very astute financial planner. At one point in the conversation, her husband, who is a medical professional, brings up his desire to buy a new luxury sports car in the near future.

Before the discussion gets very far, the planner brings out a chart that correlates how much the man makes per hour, less the money he pays in income tax, to help them determine how many more hours he will have to work in order to cover the cost of the new car and still stay on track with the family's financial goals. When he discovers that the real cost is going to be ten extra hours of office time a month, it helps both husband and wife put this want into perspective.

Young people would do well to understand this same principle early on. It is not until they have to do the work on their own and earn their own money that they will realize that the real cost is not the price tag, but the time, effort, and energy it takes to earn the money to cover the cost.

Action: Think of the things you can do today to help your young person realize the real value of things in terms of the time, effort and energy it takes to earn the money to buy them.

Money Matter #5: *Consider the difference between managing money versus having it manage you.*

Imagine this contrast between two young people--Rex and Rich. Rex is into everything new, " in," and very hip. He can tell you every new brand name in clothing, the best music albums to buy and the newest movie that you must see. Rex can also be heard at home constantly hounding Mom and Dad for more money for this and that. He has refined the art of persistence in this area. If he can't get it from one parent, he tries the other. His parents tire of the hounding and often just give in to his persistent requests.

Rex is a financial train wreck in the making. He is a prime target for the first credit card offer that comes his way when he gets a little older. Since money has always been "free," the offer of credit will do a lot to feed his insatiable appetite for everything new that he sees. He is bound to be a credit catfish, bouncing from one credit offer to the next, always living beyond his means with little hope of ever reaching any type of economic independence.

Rich, on the other hand, learned some very valuable money lessons early in life. His parents sat down with him before he reached his teenage years and helped him identify ways that he could earn some money of his own. They clearly drew the line between things that the family budget would cover and the other things that were his own responsibility. They even went down to the bank and opened up an account where he could deposit the money he earned.

Each month he would balance his own bank statement, see how much he was earning and spending, and figure out how he was going to manage what he had. He learned early in his life how to budget and manage his own money and that there is never a free lunch.

Moral: Rich will most likely be that--RICH! He has learned early on to manage his money and will do so throughout his life, while Rex will always be managed by his money. Which type of adult would you like to take credit for raising?

Action: Think what you can do to help your young people learn the basics of money management so they will always be in control of their money instead of having their money in control of them?

Money Matter #6: *Teach about leverage–working for money versus your money working for you.*

The first lesson in leverage in my own life came as an early teenager. Every boy in our family got a newspaper route at age twelve. It was a simple course in money management and how to run a business. We had to be reliable and deliver the "product"on time each day. In those days we had to bill the customer, go out and meet the customer face-to-face each month, collect, and then pay the newspaper company at the end of the month. We got to keep what was left. If we couldn't collect from a customer, it came straight out of our pocket, not the newspaper company's.

The experience was invaluable for a twelve year-old. But the real lesson in leverage came while mowing the neighbor's lawn!

Each week I would mow and trim Mr. Peterson's lawn as well as weed the flowerbeds. He paid me a set amount each week for the work, regardless of how many hours I spent doing it. I started working faster while keeping up the quality of the work. I added a few more customers at the same fee. When things got going, it was not hard to figure out that I could get some other boys to help me out for an hourly rate, get more done and still make money.

Imagine all of the work values that were learned as well as the lessons in leverage. I soon realized that all jobs are not created equal. There is a big difference between working for an hourly wage and working for an end result. Leverage comes from results, not just from putting in time.

Money leverage: One of our sessions at Eagle "U" centers around the power of time and compound interest--getting your money to work for you instead of just working for money. Financial institutions have produced some very revealing graphics that illustrate this. They are associated with Individual Retirement Accounts (IRA's). Banks have made the comparison between the person who begins at age 19 to save and invest $2,000 a year and the one who starts at age 29 to do the same thing. The one beginning at 19 can stop investing after 10 years and have more at age 65 than the one who begins at age 29 and continues to save the $2,000 a year for 30 years. The failure to learn this principle makes the difference between realizing the dream of financial independence and arriving at retirement age with little or nothing to retire on. (See chart on page 182-183.)

Consider how early in your young people's experience they will have the opportunity to learn the lessons of leverage at work--the power of making their money work for them instead of just working for money. They will then begin to think in a whole different way about the value of being productive, about having people on their work force instead of being part of one. On their way up the career ladder they will develop a management point of view. That attitude is so uncommon that those who have it are soon identified and are given increased opportunities.

IRA Savings Plan Comparison

Year	Age	Annual Contribution	Year-end Value	Age	Annual Contribution	Year-end Value
1	19	2,000	2,260	19	0	
2	20	2,000	4,814	20	0	
3	21	2,000	7,700	21	0	
4	22	2,000	10,961	22	0	
5	23	2,000	14,645	23	0	
6	24	2,000	18,809	24	0	
7	25	2,000	23,515	25	0	
8	26	2,000	26,831	26	0	
9	27	0	32,579	27	2,000	2,260
10	28	0	36,815	28	2,000	4,814
11	29	0	41,601	29	2,000	7,700
12	30	0	47,009	30	2,000	10,961
13	31	0	53,120	31	2,000	14,645
14	32	0	60,026	32	2,000	18,809
15	33	0	67,829	33	2,000	23,515
16	34	0	76,647	34	2,000	28,831
17	35	0	86,611	35	2,000	34,839
18	36	0	97,870	36	2,000	41,629
19	37	0	110,593	37	2,000	49,300
20	38	0	124,970	38	2,000	57,969
21	39	0	141,217	39	2,000	67,765
22	40	0	159,575	40	2,000	78,835
23	41	0	180,319	41	2,000	91,343
24	42	0	203,761	42	2,000	105,478
25	43	0	230,250	43	2,000	121,450

Year	Age	Annual Contribution	Year-end Value	Age	Annual Contribution	Year-end Value
26	44	0	260,182	44	2,000	139,499
27	45	0	294,006	45	2,000	159,894
28	46	0	332,227	46	2,000	182,940
29	47	0	375,416	47	2,000	208,982
30	48	0	424,221	48	2,000	238,410
31	49	0	479,396	49	2,000	271,663
32	50	0	541,687	50	2,000	309,239
33	51	0	612,107	51	2,000	351,700
34	52	0	691,680	52	2,000	399,681
35	53	0	781,599	53	2,000	453,900
36	54	0	803,207	54	2,000	515,167
37	55	0	998,024	55	2,000	584,398
38	56	0	1,127,767	56	2,000	662,630
39	57	0	1,274,376	57	2,000	751,034
40	58	0	1,440,045	58	2,000	850,926
41	59	0	1,627,251	59	2,000	963,807
42	60	0	1,830,794	60	2,000	1,091,352
43	61	0	2,077,837	61	2,000	1,235,499
44	62	0	2,347,956	62	2,000	1,398,171
45	63	0	2,653,190	63	2,000	1.582,422
46	64	0	2,998,105	64	2,000	1,790,397
47	65	0	3,307,858	65	2,000	2,025,408
		16,000	<16,000>		78,000	<78,000>
			3,291,858			1,947,408
			3,371,850			

The Vision

One of our visions at Eagle "U" is to help young people get a seven-year head start in their careers and their lives. We do that by giving them systems whereby they can determine earlier in life the career that fits them so they don't have to go through years of catfish-style trial and error trying to find their place in the world.

What a tragedy when a young person picks a career just because it makes a lot of money. What an equal tragedy when a career choice is made with no regard to money. It's all a balance.

The Money Matters Action Checklist

Help your young person gain these realistic perspectives about money:

❏ Most things in life are privileges and privileges must be earned.

❏ There is a need to distinguish between needs and wants, and a need for opportunities to earn the wants.

❏ Immediate gratification comes with a price. Ownership has its privileges.

❏ The real value of what things cost is measured in terms of the time, effort and energy it takes to earn the money.

❏ Stay in control of your money or your money will get control of you.

❏ Using leverage is the fastest way to improve earning power.

❏ There is a big difference between making your money work for you and just working for money.

MISTAKE 13
Thinking One Size Fits All

Walking down the hallway of a suburban Pittsburgh hotel after a lunch break several years ago, I stopped to make a quick call home before going back into the seminar where I was presenting to a large group of professionals from the area.

My wife, Cheryl, answered the phone and immediately reported some exciting news: "Honey, we're pregnant again." She was on her way home from the doctor's office where she had had an ultrasound. "What was especially interesting," she continued, "was when the doctor started talking about the 'other baby.'"

"What other baby? Was he talking about one of the two we already have?" I asked.

"No. The two we are about to get!"

Every birth in our family has been a miracle and that was doubly so with the birth of our identical twins girls. I'll never forget the feeling of overwhelming wonder I had as I stood in the delivery room looking at the two isolettes labeled "Baby A" and "Baby B." The twins looked exactly alike. Their height and weight were only fractions apart. They were absolutely perfect in every way except one - they didn't come with an owner's manual!

Because of their identical appearance, it would have been very easy that day to have made the mistake of thinking that they were of a singular make and model.

Time has proven that inside of those two miracles are very distinct little people with their own likes and dislikes, fears, motivations and personalities. Even though they are both the same size, what fits each of them in everything but clothing is very different.

Similarly, every young person we work with is different. So while this entire book has been filled with ideas and prescriptions, this last chapter comes with a final warning: **One size does not fit all.**

There is not any one thing that works with all people all of the time. People are too different. What works with one may have no impact on another. Because of this, please beware of the following three one-make, one-model, one-size-fits-all traps that seem to sneak into our attitudes when dealing with young people:

1. Thinking No Assembly Is Required

Christmas Eve must be one of the most frustrating nights of the year for young Dads everywhere. At the eleventh hour, after the kids are tucked in bed, Dad can be found out in the garage, in the basement or in some other remote part of the house assembling all of the toys that have to be put together for Christmas morning. I don't know who the genius is who educated the writers of the directions for most children's toys because in most cases it would take at least a graduate engineer to understand them.

Imagine my glee one Christmas Eve to discover that most of the toys had prominently printed on the outside of their boxes "No Assembly Required." It was the most enjoyable Christmas Eve to date!

In the adult search for less stress, more enjoyment and less hassle, it is easy to slip into a "No Assembly Required" attitude toward young people.   It usually shows up in attempting to motivate teenagers which is a desire most parents have.

Here is an account of an interchange I had with the mother of a 15 year-old boy:

Mom: I just want him to be more motivated.

Me: What does he like to do?

Mom: Play video games and watch T.V.

Me: What other interests does he have?

Mom: Hanging out with his friends.

Me: How does he feel about school?

Mom: He never studies, so he is pretty disinterested.

Me: What is his biggest goal?

Mom: I have no idea. He doesn't have one.

Me: What is his biggest fear?

Mom: I don't know. He would never tell me anything like that.

Me: When was the last time the two of you did something
        together?

Mom: He just wants to be with his friends.

One of the biggest struggles can be staying in touch and staying connected to a young person. It would be nice if they were all motivated by the same things that motivate us or the same things that motivate their siblings, but that is simply not the case. Each one is different and is motivated by different things. There is no one size that fits all, and so there is a tremendous amount of assembly required in terms of time, attention, listening, and observing.

2. Failing to Understand That There Will Be No Warranty Recall Notice

In a discussion with the father of a troubled young man, the father said, "I've tried everything I know and nothing has worked with the boy. God made him so I'm turning him back over to God to help him."

Several weeks later in a follow-up conversation with the father, an inquiry was made as to how the boy was doing. The father replied, "I turned him over to God, but He's not doing much better with the boy than I did!"

Wouldn't it be nice at times if there were a recall center where you could send your young people to have all the problems fixed that occur along the way in their lives?

There obviously is no such place. Yet far too often we see young people who are turned over to figurative recall centers with the hope that they will get the help, direction and focus they need. Some of those imaginary recall centers include:

* school teachers,
* athletic coaches,
* school counselors,
* psychologists,
* church leaders and teachers,
* and community program leaders.

While all of these may provide good direction and a positive environment, none will ever replace a parent's direction and the positive influence of the family.

In high school I got involved with a school program to help students stay off drugs and alcohol. My involvement expanded to the state and finally to the national level. It was a worthwhile cause that was meant to do good and I'm sure accomplished that goal to a degree.

The wake-up call for me came one afternoon as I sat at lunch with an advertising executive who wanted to find out more about what we were doing since he was creating a publicity campaign with similar objectives. I told him about all of the extensive school-based initiatives we had designed that were being implemented all over the country. He listened with interest and then he asked, "Steve, do you really think all of those programs will solve the real problem?"

Without saying another word I knew exactly what he was talking about. The problem was not in the schools or out in the community. The problem started at home. His powerful message to me that day was that until we could go to the source of the problem, the problem would never really be solved.

While outside influences are important and can provide great reinforcement and support, there is nothing that can or will replace the influence of exemplary parents who stay connected to their children from birth on through their entire lives to provide an emotionally safe home where they can learn, grow and be loved.

3. Looking Always for a Quick Fix

In talking with parents, it is easy to pick up on who is into the quick fix mentality. It can be detected by such questions as:

"Can you get him to study more?"

"Can you give her some career direction?"

"Can you get him motivated?"

Somewhere in all of those "can you" questions is an underlying attitude that says, "If you could get that done for me, it would really relieve me from having to do it."

Unfortunately there is no quick fix for the growth, development and nurturing of a human being. Yes, support, encouragement and positive environment can be provided, but it is never an overnight process.

Beware of These "One Size Fits All" Traps

1. Thinking no assembly is required and that your young people will get the idea sooner or later and will raise themselves.

2. Failing to understand that there will be no warranty recall notice. This is thinking that there is a solution out there somewhere that will replace the influence they should be getting at home.

3. Looking always for the quick fix. This is thinking that there is some magical solution that will immediately solve the problem without time, attention, love and patience.

SOLUTION

If there is any one message that I would like to leave with parents everywhere it is this: **All young people are unique.** They have their own desires, motivations and dreams.

The solution lies in getting to know who they really are, finding out what makes them tick, and then being their most helpful cheerleaders and coaches while helping them achieve worthwhile goals. Don't leave that job to anyone else. It is one of your biggest responsibilities. Follow through, follow up, spend the time, and make the investment. Love them when they are unlovable. Help them to find their own unique gifts and to discover what contribution they can make to the world. Then they won't have to live a frustrated life as a "catfish" bumping from one job to another, from one relationship to another, with little direction or positive focus on where they are really going.

Our goal at Eagle "U" is to support that effort. We would never think of ourselves as a replacement for what is going on at home. We can increase the progress, open the mind, expand the thinking and help young people get a seven-year head start in life, but not without the support of great parents and other mentors.

After All You Can Do

The experience of meeting young people in a totally unique atmosphere has provided a laboratory that is priceless. Eagle "U" is certainly not a replacement for prudent parenting, but it often brings out latent talents and validates things that parents have tried diligently to advocate. The examples of developing hidden potential are numerous.

Let me share just a few significant examples. Each one of these true stories from Eagle "U" is individual and different.   In each instance, a life was touched in a very unique way that made a significant contribution to the direction of the individual. Each of these events came about because of caring people who took the time to make the difference in a young person's life in the specific way that the individual needed the most. As a result, parents, mentors and friends could follow up, support and direct each of these young people to a bright future.

A Triggering Event: Each student who comes to Eagle "U" must pass an interview in which we make sure he or she is qualified to attend the program. We look for high achievers with open minds who want to learn and grow. Sometimes these qualities are hidden deep inside and not easily seen on the surface.

Such was the case with Rick. He was a quiet, somewhat introverted young man who had suffered a nervous breakdown early in his youth. His communication with his parents was limited, and he didn't have many friends. With some reservations we accepted Rick into Eagle "U," assigned him to a great group of other students with one of our best team leaders.

Over the days that followed, it became apparent that he had been accepted as an equal in his group and was beginning to imitate their more extroverted characteristics. He began to open up and participate. He made some new friends, and from them and his leader he gained a whole new perspective of what he could do with his life. We felt good about his progress, but had no idea what would happen when he returned to the environment in which he had been raised.

The Monday morning after Rick's return home, we got a call from his parents. They told of their son's arrival at the airport. The first thing he did was give them both a big hug and thank them for what they had done for him. He talked with them non-stop until three o'clock in the morning. They communicated more in those hours right after his return home than they had in the previous three years combined. From that day forward with his parents as his biggest confidants, Rick transformed his life. He became an outstanding student, made high quality friends, and has gone on to a bright career.

Rick's experience is just one example of many where a simple triggering event ignited the confidence and genius inside. With parental guidance and follow through from that point on, his life was off in a whole new direction.

A Realization: Ted came to Eagle "U" as one of the brightest young high school students we had ever met. His vocabulary was extensive. He was incredibly well read. He had perfect grades and was seriously focused.

On the last day of the program, we hold a public speaking contest where the students prepare and present a short speech in which they have the opportunity to share what they have learned at Eagle "U" and what they are going to do with that new knowledge.

Ted was voted best speaker in his group, so he went on to speak in front of all of the students at the conclusion of the course.

I sat and watched in amazement as this young man, whom we had gotten to know as the supreme intellect of the group, shared his thoughts about what had happened to him during the week.

He talked of how he came in with an attitude of superiority. He said he had not felt he had much in common with others his age because very few had achieved what he had. As a result he did not have very many friends. He confessed that he had had no close friends at all up until the time he came to the course.

He told of how the other students had helped him make what he considered to be the greatest discovery of his life - that life was about people and relationships, not just about grade point and the accumulation of knowledge. Being with a totally new group of young people, all of whom had their own perspectives, gave him what he described as "a whole new life."

Two days later, Ted's father called in tears. He said, "You've given me back my son." He went on to explain that he and Ted had not had a very meaningful relationship for the past couple of years. Ted had shut his father out like he had most all other people in his life. When Ted got home, he told his father about his experience and that the first relationship he wanted back in his life was with his dad. Today, Ted's dad is his most valued mentor.

A Life Saved: Paul came to Eagle "U" with the sponsorship of his aunt who cared for him very much and was very concerned about his future. Paul was from a broken home. His father had committed suicide after the divorce, and his mother did not relate to Paul.

With this as a home setting, it would be easy to understand that Paul did not interact easily with others. He kept to himself. He would not even walk with his group during the first two days despite his group's efforts to include him.

I was concerned about him and whether he was getting much out of the program. That concern changed to my amazement late on the second day. We were just getting started on a group exercise that required the students to be in teams of two. With no prompting from the instructors, a very outgoing and attractive young lady, who had been Miss South Carolina U.S.A., went over to Paul and asked if she could be his partner. He probably felt intimidated but also must have felt validated. As they worked together and she showed genuine interest in him, his attitude started to change and he began to open up to the group.

Paul was asked by his group to represent them on the last day and give his speech to all the students. Paul revealed to the group his troubled past and that he had almost given up all hope in life and in other people by the time he arrived earlier in the week. He shared how the people in his group had befriended him, made him feel important and had given him some hope. "In fact," he said, "you have saved my life."

What came in as a discouraged, directionless "catfish" left as a focused, goal oriented, motivated young man who had a new direction in life. Like all of us, Paul just needed a little hope, a little direction, some friends, and some good mentors to put him on the path to success.

That is what we hope for all young people - that they can get the direction and the focus early in life that will help them get a seven-year head start on their careers, whatever they may be.

While we hope we make a contribution in that direction, we know that parents have the strongest influence on the lives of their young people. **You are the first line of defense.**

I personally hope that by knowing what the **13 biggest mistakes parents make** are and avoiding them, that parents can build a foundation for their young people that will give them a powerful start. It is the parents who can help young people avoid life as directionless "catfish" who just swim along bumping into things and hoping a new direction will be better than the last. Parents can make the difference that will give young people the direction, the hope and the vision they need to succeed.

Make it happen!